T0318197

THE ECONOMICS OF SERVICES

THE
ECONOMICS
OF
SERVICES

Edited by
GARY AKEHURST
and
JEAN GADREY

Routledge
Taylor & Francis Group

LONDON AND NEW YORK

First published 1987 by
FRANK CASS AND COMPANY LIMITED

Published 2023 by Routledge
4 Park Square, Milton Park, Abingdon, Oxon OX14 4RN
605 Third Avenue, New York, NY 10017

Routledge is an imprint of the Taylor & Francis Group, an informa business

British Library Cataloguing in Publication Data
The Economics of services.
1. Service industries
I. Akehurst, Gary   II. Gadrey, Jean
III. Service industries journal
338.4   HD9980.5

This group of studies first appeared in a Special Issue on 'The Economics of Services' of *The Service Industries Journal*, Vol.7, No.4, published by Frank Cass & Co. Ltd.

ISBN 13: 978-0-7146-3337-4 (pbk)

Contents

Editors' Preface

Most of the papers in this collection are revised versions of those given at the international conference 'Dynamics of Services and Economic Theories' organised by the ERMES research group at the University of Lille I on 30 January 1987.

The editors sincerely thank for their support:

the French Ministry of Research (Technologie–Emploi–Travail Programme)
the Region Nord-Pas-de-Calais
the University of Lille I
and the National Centre for Scientific Research (IFRESI, Lille).

We should also like to thank for their support for the organisation of the colloquium and for their helpful comments:

Jacques de Bandt (Research Director, CNRS)
Pierre Strobel (Ministry of Research)
Jean-Claude Delaunay (Commissariat Général du Plan and University of Lille I)
and Alfred Sauvy (Professor at the Collège de France).

Another set of papers stemming from the same conference is planned to be published in France in 1988, on the topics of producer services, social and spatial division of labour in service industries.

GARY AKEHURST
JEAN GADREY

Notes on the Contributors

Gary Akehurst is Professor and Head of the Department of Catering and Hotel Management, Dorset Institute of Higher Education, UK. He is also a founding editor of *The Service Industries Journal*. Previously he was a member of Faculty of the University of Wales Institute of Science and Technology, the University of Surrey and Manchester Polytechnic. Professor Akehurst's research and publications have generally been in the area of corporate strategies and market structure in the hotel and retail industries.

Jean Gadrey is an economist at the University of Lille I, France. Dr Gadrey is the author of several papers and books on services economics; the editor of the journal *Cahiers Lillois d'Economie et de Sociologie* and the director of a research group on service economics (ERMES).

Bernard Delmas is an economist at the University of Lille I, France. From 1976 to 1985 he led the Regional Department of CEREQ (Centre d'Etudes et de Recherches sur les Qualifications) in Lille.

Hilary Silver is Assistant Professor of Sociology and Urban Studies at Brown University in Providence, Rhode Island, USA. Her forthcoming book, *Winners and Losers: Income Inequality and Urban Economies*, examines the impact on income distribution of shifts from manufacturing to services in large American metropolitan areas. Professor Silver has also written about state-level industrial policy in the USA; the sale of public housing; and paid work performed in the home.

Edith Archambault is Professor of Economics at the University of Poitiers, France. Her research activities take place at the Laboratoire d'Economie Sociale of the University of Paris I, and currently deal with accounting for non-market items: environment, home production, voluntary work, the underground economy and the economics of culture.

Jonathan Gershuny is Professor of Sociology at the University of Bath, UK. He was formerly a Senior Fellow at the Science Policy Research Unit of the University of Sussex. Among his previous publications are *Social Innovation and the Division of Labour* (1983) and (with Ian Miles) *The New Service Economy* (1983).

Gonzales d'Alcantara is Research Director of the European Cooperation Fund and Professor of Econometrics at the University of Antwerp (UFSIA). He has been the scientific co-ordinator of the European Seminar on 'Concepts of Productivity in the Services' held in December 1985 at the Catholic University of Louvain and sponsored by the FAST programme of the European Communities. Dr d'Alcantara has written several papers on services economics.

Pieter Tordoir is an economic geographer responsible for the research on tertiary economic development at the Research Centre for Urban and Regional Planning–TNO in Delft, the Netherlands. Dr Tordoir's main research themes are the internationalisation of service markets; the market dynamics of advanced producer services, professionalisation within industry and the role of services in regional development. He is engaged in the Johns Hopkins University international services project at Lille, France. Other fields for research and consultancy include industrial restructuring, technological change and urban and regional development.

Piet Coppieters is Associate Professor of Economics in the Faculty of Applied Economics, University of Antwerp (UFSIA). For the past ten years he has been researching the development of employment in the service industries and the economics of technological change. Professor Coppieters has written several articles on the economics of services, the impact of new technology on employment and labour market problems.

Olivier Ruyssen is at present at the EEC Commission where he participates in the FAST programme (Forecasting and Assessment in Science and Technology), Directorate General for Science, Research and Development. Dr Ruyssen is in charge of the Services and Technological Change programme. Besides various papers he has published *Les échanges Internationaux* (1978), *Old World and New Technologies* (with M. Godet) in the series 'European Perspectives'; and is also joint author of *Eurofutures – the Challenges of Innovation* (1984).

Orio Giarini is an economist who is chiefly concerned with economic analysis and research related to the service sector. He is a member of the Club of Rome, Professor of Economics at the Graduate Institute of European Studies of the University of Geneva and chairman of the European section of the International Science Policy Foundation. Professor Giarini has published widely on the economics of services.

Jean Rémy Roulet is Research Fellow, PROGRES (Research Programme on the Service Economy) of the Geneva Association. He is also Editor of the PROGRES newsletter published by the Geneva Association. Dr Roulet is the author of several papers on the economics of services.

The Economics of Services: An Introduction

by

Gary Akehurst

This introduction examines certain issues concerning the economics of services and introduces the articles in this special collection. The collection represents the current 'state of the art' of the economic analysis of services.

As a discipline economics has been slow to take up the challenge which is now posed by the development of predominantly service-based economies in the developed world. Despite the undeniable evidence of the contribution of marketed services to both formal employment and GNP in many countries many economists have yet to recognise this, whether in theoretical or empirical researches. Tordoir, writing in one of the papers in this collection, considers that economists can be divided into three camps:

- those who have yet to recognise services (both formal and informal, marketed and unmarketed) as a legitimate field of research study and theory development;
- those working on the study of services utilising existing theoretical frameworks (but not in any significant way changing this existing and traditional framework);
- those adapting the existing theoretical framework and developing new methods of interpretation.

This collection of papers is from economists who, having acknowledged the fundamental importance of services to our societies today, are actually attempting to reverse the indifference and, let it be said, ignorance surrounding a whole series of economic and non-economic transactions. Of course, the concept of a 'service' is unusually complex – it brings problems of quantifying output, of value-added, of relative prices, of intangibility, of defining service occupations, of intermediate and final consumption, of the fact that a consumer of a service is also an active agent in its production, that many service transactions are unique and cannot be replicated, and so on. This very complexity surely cannot be that intimidating? We should, however, proceed with caution: '. . . such is the diversity of the service sector that it defies applications of a principal theory, a particular analytical method, or a dominant mode of interpretation' [Daniels, 1985: xvi]. Daniels was referring primarily to the development of a geography of services. The question is whether this statement could equally be applied to other disciplines such as economics or indeed the whole spectrum of academic enquiry.

The present collection is proof that the very heterogeneity and diversity of the service sector should not be allowed to detract from the essential task of attempting to construct a systematic and rigorous theoretical framework to underpin and stimulate empirical investigations of both a macro and micro nature. Although these papers are essentially economics- or social science-based, a recurring theme is the need to develop an integrated, inter-disciplinary approach involving several disciplines such as economics, sociology, marketing, management and geography. This offers both a challenge and a problem. The challenge is clear: we must understand the processes, operations, industries and organisations of that sector of the economy which is providing employment for a substantial majority of the population in many developed countries and contributing an ever-increasing proportion of gross national product. The problem is that very few researchers are applying themselves to this task and those who are could well be constrained by the traditional (and one begins to feel not altogether appropriate) methodologies of individual disciplines. The limitations of a single discipline approach to services will be apparent when reading these papers. As if these criticisms were not enough, the problems are compounded by an apparent lack of knowledge of what is happening in other disciplines with respect to the analysis of services. This is resulting in a duplication of efforts and a tendency to get caught in the 'time-warp' of developing ever more complex taxonomies and definitions of what constitutes a 'service' and what are the parameters of 'the formal service sector' and 'informal service sector'.

CONSOLIDATION AND THE NEED TO ADVANCE BEYOND THE
'DEFINITIONS' PHASE

While the development of taxonomies is important, we must recognise that this is but the first step in research and should never be an end in itself. Research which does little more than list the apparent characteristics of services, without going on to consider the *managerial* and *economic* implications of these characteristics, is frankly a waste of time and resources. The words 'apparent characteristics' are used because very often they are little more than preconceived, self-selected features which the researcher, in his or her experience as a consumer, believes to be distinguishing features of services compared with goods. The following list is often reproduced:

1. services are intangible and cannot be stored
2. consumption and production are generally simultaneous and inseparable
3. the benefits of services are difficult to describe
4. the consumer is a central element in the transfer and exchange process
5. lack of homogeneity and problems in controlling the quality of services

A 'service', then, it is argued, can be defined with reference to these necessary and sufficient characteristics or conditions. This functional approach sometimes argues that *all* these characteristics should be present when distinguishing goods from services; at other times it is argued that only *some* of these features should be present.What can be certain, however, is that the functional approach does not resolve the thorny question of what is or is not a 'service'. As Blois (1983: 115-116) rightly points out, 'it is not absolutely clear or obvious which of these characteristics must apply to a product before it is considered to be "a service"'. Blois again: 'While such a situation exists there remains the obvious danger that "a service" is no more than that to which an observer chooses to apply the label "service"' [Blois, 1983: 144].

Clearly, all services do not have the same characteristics in all circumstances, nor are these characteristics necessarily the sole preserve of services. Nightingale introduces a logical approach, with reference to the hospitality industry, which is inter-disciplinary and provides a bridge between definitions, management of service activities and marketing considerations:

> The main subdivisions of the service sector are 'services for individuals' and 'services for organisations'. Each of these can be divided by the type of service, for example, person-related services such as air travel and hairdressing; product-related services such as retailing and car hire; information-related services such as telephones and radio; financial services such as banking and insurance.
>
> The hospitality industry provides a number of product-related services, for example, car-parking and laundry services, and supplies ancillary goods through in-house shops and cigarette dispensers, etc. But these are secondary to the main objects of providing rooms and meals which are primarily person-related services for individuals. Consumption of hospitality services generally involves four elements:
> (a) direct consumption of physical goods, such as food in a restaurant
> (b) use of physical facilities such as buildings and furniture
> (c) interactions with the persons providing the service and often other customers
> (d) information about the service [Nightingale, 1985: 10-11].

What makes Nightingale's approach worthy of study is not so much the definition of services by destination of output (that is, consumer/producer services, final and intermediate products [see also Greenfield, 1966]) but by bringing together the supply and demand sides with a particular focus on the interaction between supplier and customer, that is, *the delivery system* (the mechanism of placing the 'product [involving both physical and intangible/psychological elements] before customers and the *role* of customers [the needs, desires, expectations and participation of the customer]. This involves a supply process, an active consumer involvement and an eventual service outcome. The examination of the matching and mis-matching of supply and demand, the fundamental role of the consumer and the allocative mechanism of price requires not just an economic approach, nor just marketing management – it also requires an understanding of psychology and social processes. In short, an inter-disciplinary approach is imperative to truly understanding a multi-faceted but essentially economic transaction.

One final quote from Nightingale:

> To say that a service is person-related means that its main objective is to bring about some change of state in the customer, or to maintain an existing state, which for one reason or another he is unable to do for himself, or chooses not to. Thus, an airline transports passengers from, say, New York to London; a barber cuts hair; and a hotel provides rest and refreshment. These examples all exhibit the other key characteristic of person-related services, which is that the customer is inextricably involved in the process of providing them. Indeed, the process is frequently as much a part of the service as its outcome [Nightingale, 1985: 10].

Marketing researchers may have the right approach in that the generic term should be 'products', with services constituting a subset [Middleton, 1983]. Foxall [1984] suggests however, that the appropriate generic concept is surely that of a *service*:

> ... the suggestion that a single conceptual basis should be found for both 'products' and 'services' is sound in view of the fact that customers are interested in obtaining the same thing – benefits, satisfactions or services – whether or not they are supplied via a physical entity ... Marketing analysts should recognise that that which is exchanged for customers' money in a market transaction is a *service* (or a bundle of services) which may or may not involve the transfer of a physical entity' [Foxall, 1984: 2].

Some marketing writers [notably Shostack, 1977 and Gronroos, 1980] take up the delivery mechanism in relation to classifying products along a continuum according to degrees of intangibility or tangibility; but generally the discipline of marketing is moving in a direction which could usefully be considered by other disciplines in the majority of cases. The case is this: consumers purchase and consume services (in the generic-benefits-needs sense) 'irrespective of the mechanism by which they are generated and supplied' [Foxall, 1984: 3]. We observe differences both within and between 'services' and 'products' but do not force these observations to fit a spurious analytical dichotomy [Foxall, 1984: 3]. There are signs that economists are moving in this direction as well, for Giarini and Roulet in their article [116] state: 'In a service economy what is bought is the functioning of an object or a system, and no longer the object itself'.

It is clear that many marketing writers view the 'marketing of services' as but a temporary area of study, useful at present to correct the over-concentration on manufacturing activities but one which should not destroy the overall unity of the discipline of marketing, that is, once the services-manufacturing imbalance has been corrected to take account of economic realities then the sub-area of services marketing will be re-absorbed into mainstream marketing. We would venture to suggest that the discipline of economics (and other disciplines) could for some, but not all, purposes avoid the spurious distinction between products and services, and in so doing actually advance the frontiers of knowledge. Sometimes economics has found itself in ludicrous situations where the existing methodologies just cannot cope with person-related services or product-related services [Akehurst, 1982] whereas, if economics had taken a 'products' approach (that is, a consumer utility–benefits–demand–supply interaction approach) greater advances might have been made to date.

However, this is certainly not to deny that certain definitions, parameters and classifications do have an important role to play provided clear objectives have been set. It would be wrong to deny the usefulness of the standard industrial classification approach in certain circumstances or the identification of pre and post industrial societies or a perishability–durability–utility goods approach but the point is that economics as a discipline, for example, has often failed to take combined supply and demand approach, ironic really when one remembers that it was economics which introduced the world to these fundamental concepts and the importance of the interaction of these two forces for the successful operation of free market economies.

A definition, therefore, should be for a purpose; it should serve as the servant of future research, not enslave and constrain that research. Neither should the search for classifications and categories be an end in itself for that results not just in descriptive generalisations but also diverts valuable research resources away from the real problems such as the measurement of service sector productivity or the profitable and efficient operation of service organisations and businesses. An example of a working definition with a specific purpose is that developed for *The Service Industries Journal*:

> ... the unifying theme is *service industries* which are taken to be those organisations and businesses which (regardless of ownership, profit/non-profit orientation and employee occupations) produce, and are inextricably bound up with the consumption process of, generally intangible products; where the consumer (whether individual or business is a central, fundamental component of the whole transfer and exchange process. Therefore, these service industries can be defined both in terms of supply/production characteristics and demand/consumption characteristics. We do not suggest, however, that the definition of service industries is capable of easy solution but we believe the above statement is a useful working definition ... The definition above recognises, however, that services can be, and are, intricately tied with material goods; that service-based organisations are often involved in the sale of material goods and use material goods and facilities in the pursuit of their goals – like retailing for instance. In addition, we recognise that service

occupations are to be found in manufacturing businesses (and vice versa) but there can be no denying that service *industries* can be identified (however imprecisely) and that they are ripe for investigation . . . . As subsets of the industry set (defined on both a supply and demand basis) one is inevitably forced to consider first, the meaning of 'service'; second, the nature, development and organisation of service products as the main output of service industries; and third, the characteristics and organisation of service personnel (and non-service personnel) within service industries but recognising that service occupations exist outside definable service industries. This is not to deny that a service element forms part of the 'product' of most industries but a line has to be drawn somewhere, otherwise the journal can be fairly accused of casting its net far too widely [Editorial, *Service Industries Journal,* 1985; see also Minter, 1987].

Consolidation involves unification and the creation of a domain of study. We may accept that the study of the service sector is a temporary phenomenon necessary to redress the overwhelming bias towards manufacturing activities and before re-absorption into mainstream academic thought and activity. On the other hand, one may argue that study of the service sector and its diverse activities is a legitimate and quite separate activity. Whichever viewpoint is taken (and both have attractions) consolidation means taking stock of what research has successfully taken place to date and what research is in progress. It also means marrying the theoretical with the empirical and encouraging the cross-fertilisation of ideas between disciplines (that is, integration).

Gershuny and Miles have noted: '. . .despite the massive expansion of service employment in recent decades, despite awareness of the changing prospects for job creation in the services – despite all these things, research into the services is far from forming a coherent whole' [Gershuny and Miles, 1983: 10]. How much longer will researchers continue to carry out their work on services and the service sector with little or no recognition of and willingness to use concepts and ideas developed in other disciplines? Until this essential point is realised services research will continue to operate in what could be described as 'the dark ages'.

Bearing in mind the foregoing points the economic analysis of services has undergone two distinct phases. First, the model of economic development, where an economy moves from being predominantly agriculturally-based to manufacturing-based (the industrial revolution phase) finally moving to a predominantly services-based economy (post-industrial society phase). This transition is seen as a maturing feature. This model of economic development once fashionable and widely quoted is now known to have been somewhat of an over-simplification. The second phase of economic analysis, concentrating on households as both production and consumption units with respect to services has been a major stimulator of research activity. Households demand time-saving final consumer services but as income rises so there may be a tendency to replace this demand for final services by goods and the household's own labour, that is, the internalisation of services or self-services. This is familiar ground for economics – the relative prices of goods and services, the utility maximising mix of leisure and work (income) together with the scarcity of time (paid/unpaid work); purchasing of time and the conflict between consumption and leisure). These trade-offs link the *external* decisions or choices of households to *internal* decisions or choices relating to domestic work and leisure. Many of the articles in this volume rightly continue to explore this rich vein of research, which integrates economic analysis with socio-institutional analysis. However, two qualifications need to be borne in mind. First, there is clearly a limit to self-service (which can often be grossly inefficient) because of, for example, capital requirements and the possession of specialised skills. Second, employment in service industries continues to grow both relatively and absolutely due to household demand despite lower productivity. This alone suggests that self-service is not the major element in economic development but must be considered together with the growth of intermediate services provided by firms for other producers and the growth of firms which undeniably can be classifed as service producers.

Consolidation, integration and striking out in new directions (if this is needed) are essentially sequential activities. Before we can head in new directions we need to know from whence we have come and what has been done to date and thereafter, endeavour to understand how all this is related (the coherent whole approach).

Recently it has been encouraging to see studies of the measurement of output of services and productivity in services [see for example, Fletcher and Snee, 1985; Bonamy and Barcet, 1986 and Gadrey, 1986]. Such work is of particular importance and deserves our support. Rarely however, has there been work of a macro-economic nature in terms of the implication of the growth of services for economic growth and economic management. No one to our knowledge has explored the implications for the management of the economies of developed countries and developing countries (especially the consequences for cyclical economic fluctuations of non-storable services and the relative recession resistance of some service industries such as tourism).

We do not believe we yet know what services research is being carried out across the world, where and by whom. Until we do know with some degree of confidence what research is in progress, what research has been completed and the worth of such research, it would be presumptuous to outline 'possible new directions', for how do we know what constitutes a 'new direction', or indeed whether such a reorientation is required; and yet we have tentatively suggested earlier in this introduction that, in our view, service researchers need to:

- develop, if at all possible, a systematic and rigorous theoretical framework of an inter-disciplinary nature. This may be impossible but it must be attempted. Researchers of different disciplines must put academic pride to one side and *collaborate, across academic discipline boundaries, across institutional boundaries and above all, across national boundaries.* This does not deny the worth of individual disciplines research, which must continue and be resourced in parallel with the development of 'the coherent whole conceptual framework'.

- recognise that taxonomies and functional definitions of services have their uses but are not a substitute for rigorous empirical research which examines the economic and managerial implications of these service characteristics. Definitions are logical facilitators, that is all; however, there is a need for some agreement on a common glossary of terms.

- recognise that we may be falling into the trap of believing that services are essentially different in all respects from products; that service businesses are essentially different from product businesses in terms of orientation, operations and delivery systems. Are they? Researchers need to uncover the very essence of a service where it is most important – the interface or interaction between the service provision or delivery and the consumer. Giarini and Roulet, in their article, stress that the advanced products of a service economy require complex and complementary promotion, distribution, maintenance, etc., clearly, services are absolutely essential for the utilisation of these products.

This volume is divided into two parts. Part One takes a micro-economic and microsocial approach, focusing particularly on households and services. Part Two takes a macro-economic approach to service activities. The editors have not attempted to impose a common style or constraint on the authors; instead we have preferred to let each article speak for itself as being indicative of current economic thinking on services. This volume can fairly claim to represent the 'state of the art' as far as the economics of services is concerned. It also does not gloss over areas where the economic analysis of services is still at a rudimentary stage for this points to future research concerns. Finally, many of the papers have been translated from the French language; it may be that during the translating and editing process the editors have not done justice to the subtle arguments or nuances of style, but we hope that the essence of each paper is there for all to see.

Bernard Delmas and Jean Gadrey propound a four-level appraisal of Gershuny's theory of self-service. They discuss the economic model of self-service, its construction and concepts, (especially that of 'service function'), society and implicit family patterns. The authors conclude that Gershuny's model is only applicable to a proportion of service industries and cannot be a foundation for a general forecasting of the future of service industries.

Hilary Silver is also rather critical of the theory of self-service, first, because US statistics show a continuing sharp growth in consumer services, and second, because the numerous time constraints on household lives lead them to resort to services to save time. Besides economic factors there is a set of very important social changes which must be considered (female labour participation, longevity, smaller households, spatial reorganisation of social life, political struggles over consumption, etc.)

Edith Archambault considers the relationship between household economics and formal economics by studying household production. She draws inspiration from classifications and techniques used for tradeable or marketed production. Professor Archambault defends the thesis of a tertiarisation of household production, showing that the internal transformations of family activity is leading to a reduction of labour in some service industries because it is leading to the promotion of job creation in new services.

Jonathan Gershuny is concerned with 'time accountancy', that is, not only the paid work time but also the unpaid work time of an individual's life and how the time allocation evolves. The originality of this paper is the consideration not only of how individuals spend and use their own time but also the use of other people's time for their own purposes. This produces a 'chain of provision' analysis based on an accounting system which distinguishes some general categories of time-use activities. On this basis trend lines become apparent in five countries for the period 1961-86. Above all, a research procedure is suggested which links the analysis of formal employment to society's way of life in the quite concrete sense of the allocation of time between alternative activities.

In Part Two Gonzales d'Alcantara proposes starting from general equilibrium theory. Services should ensure a freely working equilibrium process on the basis of information production and exchanges; the communication between agents and the contracting processes; the establishment and protection of initial factor endowments and so on. Dr d'Alcantara establishes three main functions achieved by service activities – access, regulation and foundation, which contribute to a renewing of the analysis of these activities.

Pieter Tordoir's main thesis is that some categories of services (for example, transport and trade) are ruled by goal-oriented rationality and instrumental functions, but other services, which may be more numerous, are linked to the social interaction of individuals and organisations leading to symbolic exchanges. It is felt that it is not possible to analyse these services either through functional methods or by using common economic tools. Instead we have to call upon the help of the sociology of communication (for example, Habermas' works) to understand their present development.

The contribution of Piet Coppieters is in dealing with macro-economic growth models based on the division of the economy between main sectors. He distinguishes demand-induced growth models, supply-induced and demand-supply interaction models. Baumol's unbalanced growth model is subject to an appraisal. A general weakness of these models (except for some more recent works) according to Professor Coppieters is the insufficient weight attached to the transformation of demand functions, both final and intermediate demand.

Olivier Ruyssen's article is based on some researches carried out for the FAST European Programme. First, the different forms of services and integration of new technologies (customisation vs standardisation) are considered and second, the emerging 'meta-industrialisation' of the production structure which resorts to modern services and different production organisations.Dr Ruyssen then considers the involvements of these transformations on the policies of the EEC institutions.

Orio Giarini's and Jean Rémy Roulet's contribution has two aims: first, to propound an assumption on the very beginnings of contemporary services development; second, to try to understand why economic theory has forgotten this services dimension and how it would be possible to remedy this state of affairs. Some of the most original ideas expressed are those concerning the increasing complexity of production, the diversification of demand, the emerging 'utilisation value' of goods and services and supply rigidities. Service industries appear to be the main way to reduce the rigidities of economic structure and manage risks and uncertainties – the growth of which is one of the major characteristics of developed societies.

As a conclusion Jean Gadrey assesses the macro-economic trends in the consumption of goods and services by households in France and the USA and of the share of services intended for producers This statistical exercise reveals a double dynamics of services growth, which can account for the growing complexity of production and consumption processes; the rise of risks and uncertainty to be prevented or managed and the emergence of new linkages between production and uses. finally, Dr Gadrey focuses on the all-important social relationships of services.

REFERENCES

Akehurst, G.P., 1982, 'The Economics of Retailing – a Note', *Service Industries Review*, Vol. 2, No. 2.

Blois, K.J., 1983, 'Service Marketing: Assertion or Asset?, *Service Industries Journal*, Vol. 3,

Bonamy, J., and A. Barcet, 1986, 'La Productivité dans les Services: Prospective et Limite d'un Concept', Second Annual Seminar on the Service Economy, PROGRES, Geneva, June.

Cowell, D.W., 1984, *The Marketing of Services*, London: Heinemann,

Daniels, P.W., 1985 *Service Industries. A Geographical Appraisal*, London: Methuen.

Fletcher, J., and H. Snee, 1985, 'The Need for Output Measurements in the Service Industries: a Comment', *Service Industries Journal*, Vol. 5, No.1.

Foxall, G., 1984, 'Marketing *is* Service Marketing', *Service Industries Journal*, Vol. 4 No.3. Special Issue.

Foxall, G. (ed.), 1985, *Marketing in the Service Industries*, London: Frank Cass.

Gadrey, J., 1986, 'Productivité, Output Médiat et Immédiat des Activités de Services: les Difficultés d'un Transfert de Concepts', Second Annual Seminar on the Service Economy, PROGRES, Geneva, June.

Gershuny, J., 1978, *After Industrial Society: The Emerging Self-Service Economy*, London: Macmillan.

Gershuny, J., and I. Miles, 1983, *The New Service Economy: The Transformation of Employment in Industrial Societies,* London: Frances Pinter.

Greenfield, H.I., 1966, *Manpower and the Growth of Producer Services,* New York: Columbia University Press.

Gronroos, C., 1980, 'An Applied Service Marketing Theory', *Working Paper No. 57, Swedish School of Economics and Business Administration, Helsinki.*

Lovelock, C.H., 1984, *Services Marketing,* Englewood Cliffs, NJ: Prentice-Hall.

Middleton, V.T.C., 1983, 'Product Marketing – Goods and Services Compared', *Quarterly Review of Marketing,* Vol. 8, No. 4.

Minter, A., 1987, 'The Service Industries Journal: its Ethos and Emphases', *Service Industries Journal,* Vol. 7, No. 1.

Nightingale, M., 1985, 'The Hospitality Industry: Defining Quality for a Quality Assurance Programme – a Study of Perceptions', *Service Industries Journal,* Vol. 5, No. 1.

Service Industries Journal, 1985, Editorial, Vol.5, No.1

Shostack, G.L., 1977, 'Breaking Free from Product Marketing', *Journal of Marketing,* Vol. 41, No. 2.

Stanback, T.M., 1979, *Understanding the Service Economy: Employment, Productivity, Location,* Baltimore: Johns Hopkins University Press.

Stanback, T.M., Bearse, P.J. Noyelle, T.J. and Karasek, R.A., 1981, *Services: The New Economy,* Totowa, NJ: Allanheld Osmun.

On the Substitution of Goods and Services

by

Bernard Delmas and Jean Gadrey

The authors of this article put forward an evaluation and a criticism of the economic theory of self-service at several levels: the model of consumer choice between goods and services, the assumptions and basic concepts of the theory, and its social model. They estimate that this theory can only be applied to very specific situations and therefore is often misleading in forecasting.

Since the mid-1970s, the post-industrial optimism that portrayed the growth of services as evidence of more human relations of production and consumption, transcending the constraints and the conflicts of the industrial society, has been highly questioned in the research on the service economy. In the United States, following the assumptions of Stanback [1979] and Noyelle [1983], the major tendency is to regard the sector of producer services and the 'advanced services' (which constitute the qualified and strategic proportion of the former) as the essential engine of the future development of services, the function of which would be to lead the variations of production and distribution.

In Europe, this perception is in close competition with a theory, developed in Great Britain by Gershuny [1983], which considers as only secondary the transformation of the mode of production, and which, on the contrary, centres the analysis on the technical and economic mutations of the final consumption of households – this is the theory of the self-service economy. Actually, this theory defines a real model of society, as well as a model of economic behaviour for households. In this article, this model is questioned at this double theoretical level, and not at the level of statistical investigations which have been carried out elsewhere [Gadrey, 1986].

ESSENTIAL FEATURES OF THE MODEL

The Essential Theses of the Self-Service Economy

The research conducted by Gershuny [1983] which includes some conceptual, statistical and modelling aspects, can be summarised in a few rather simple theses, leading to a vigorous repudiation of post-industrial assumptions.

According to Gershuny, the origins of the current economic transformations of developed capitalist societies are found in the behaviour and the choices of households as basic units of final demand. The latter, on the one hand according to the environment in goods and services, and on the other, to the limits of time available in the domestic sphere to use the purchased goods, dictate the choice between goods (sources of 'final type services' or 'service functions' to the extent that time of domestic work is devoted to them) and the services provided from the exterior ('formal services') which fulfil the same service functions, but do not require any time of domestic work.

Now, according to Gershuny, present society would tend to evolve, not towards the externalisation of services, and thus towards the growth of formal services to households, but rather towards the domestic internalisation of services; their transformation to self-service, in the use of for example, home laundry equipment with a correlative decrease of employment in the commercial sector of laundry and dry cleaning, or of private vehicles instead of public transport.

According to Gershuny, the explanation for this trend (surprising in view of numerous ideas inherited from post-industrial thinking) lies at an elementary economic level and has recourse to an essential argument, that is, that productivity increases faster in the industrial production of goods than in the sectors of services; the relative price of services *vis-à-vis* goods continues to increase (the data on the inflationary impact of services would confirm this) so that the solution of self-service is more advantageous compared with the reliance on formal services. As such, little by little, households turn their purchases in this direction.

In the long term, this would affect the sizeable sectors of education and health, with the development of domestic technologies, and of teaching and assisted-diagnosis softwares. The upsurge in Western economies would rely on this new wave of innovations, the core commodity of which would be the software of information technology. The hardware and the necessary networks would qualify this model of society in the same way as the infrastructures of transport and energy qualified the previous patterns of industrial societies.

But this tendential pattern of the neo-industrial economy of self-service, in as much as it is based on hypotheses about household behaviour, seems unable to do without a mathematical model as the theoretical basis for the choices made by the final consumption units. That is why Gershuny devotes an initial chapter of his more developed book [1983] to the presentation of such a model, inspired by the works of Becker [1965], Linder [1971], and Gronau [1977]. However, this chapter is original in several respects compared with these previous developments, which have had the merit of introducing, in the neo-classical theory of consumption, the time of domestic work as a variable and a budget constraint, along with the traditional income constraint.

THEORETICAL CONTEXT OF THE MODEL

The traditional theory of choice between working and leisure time, introduced by Robbins in 1930, aimed at the derivation of the consumer's supply curve for labour-time on the basis of the utility maximising mix of leisure and income (as a purchasing power for goods). While remaining within the analytical framework of the new consumption theory, the theory of choice which Becker developed in 1965, improves the basic model in two ways:

- utility is no longer a function of the amount of goods consumed but the amount of basic 'commodities'
- those commodities are provided by households by the combination of goods, services and time.

As such, the parallel is drawn with the neo-classical theory of the firm: households become real units of production of basic commodities by use of inputs (material or not) and time.

Somewhat paradoxically, however, leisure as such, which was at the core of the traditional scheme, disappears from this model, each fraction of time being devoted only to paid work or self-production of commodities. This is what leads Gronau to re-introduce it, by making a distinction between time of domestic production (domestic work) and time of domestic consumption (leisure): only the former would preferably be entrusted to someone else (if the cost were not too high). The extreme case, fairly frequent to his mind, is that where domestic and formal work are perfect substitutes. In this case, there is little difference between goods and services, whether self-produced or purchased on the market. It will be noted that for simplicity Gronau neglects marketed goods as inputs of domestic work. This weakens the model by preventing it from dealing with the efficiency of domestic work.

Conversely, Gershuny places these marketed goods at the core of his analysis: more fundamentally, he can be said to turn around the analytical perspective to this problem. Actually, he no longer aims at determining the equilibrium supply curve for work but at isolating the factors affecting the respective demands of goods and services under the constraint of time available and according to the differentials of growth in productivity and relative prices.

Even if the outlook changes, the Gershuny model nevertheless remains inspired by those of Becker and Gronau, which Gershuny improves by taking into account, on the one hand, leisure, and on the other hand, goods as inputs to domestic work. Gershuny's model is more precise but it also suffers the drawback of this quality of precision: indeed certain assumptions, carried out to their utmost consequences, lead to unresolved contradictions.

EVALUATING THE ECONOMIC MODEL

Determination of the 'Time-Budget' Constraint

The starting point of the analysis is consistent with the traditional theory of choice between working and leisure time: maximise utility $U(L,T)$ under the constraints: $T+L=24$ (if T and L are respectively the daily periods of work and leisure given in hours).

In this presentation, the scheme of preferences $U(L,T)$ is actually derived from a basic system which would represent the choice between leisure and consumed goods. Indeed, work is not sought as such, but for the consumption which its income allows. Both approaches are identical only if the prices of goods and working-time are fixed. If this is not the case, there will be a modification of the system of preferences, even if the basic system is not modified. Gershuny does not mention this preliminary difficulty which, however, makes the conclusion drawn from the close study of the evolution of relative prices very problematic.

The consumer's equilibrium is reached at the point of tangency between the constraint and an indifference curve, the laws of the mixes of work- and leisure time providing the highest level of satisfaction to households. The essential difference with the traditional model is that T represents both the time of paid work (T_f) devoted to 'formal' production and the time of unpaid work (T_i) devoted to the tasks of household production. The latter's inputs are all the goods purchased by means of the salary as well as the 'informal services' which substitute for the services directly purchased from formal suppliers.

Therefore, a second optimisation problem is studied, dealing with:
- the choice between formal and informal work;
- the allocation of the income budget between goods (G) and services (S);
- the links between these two choices, taking into account a given 'productivity' of domestic labour.

The problem can be graphically represented (see Figure 1):

- point H representing the distribution between paid work and informal work, may *a priori* move all along the line corresponding to equation $T = T_f + T_i$ (whose position has been determined by the first optimisation fixing the value of T);
- the choice of T_f determines the corresponding income from labour (line $W = w.T_f$ where w is the hourly wage) and, thus, the traditional budget constraint $W = S + G$ (line MN of the first quadrant);
- *a priori* again, point P representing the shares of the two kinds of expenditure can move all along segment MN, from N where the whole income is spent on services ($S = W$) to M where it is fully spent on goods ($G = W$).
- this is where the relation between the expenditure on goods and the informal work needed for their consumption comes into play: that relation is supposed to be strictly proportional: $G = \dfrac{T_i}{p}$ (p = fixed coefficient).
- for a given position of H, one single point P of MN enables the time of corresponding informal labour to be used up, i.e., where the abscissa $G = \dfrac{T_i}{p}$ (from which the expenditure in corresponding formal services: $S = W - G$).

FIGURE 1

CHOICE BETWEEN PAID WORK AND INFORMAL WORK, EXPENDITURE IN
SERVICES AND EXPENDITURE IN GOODS

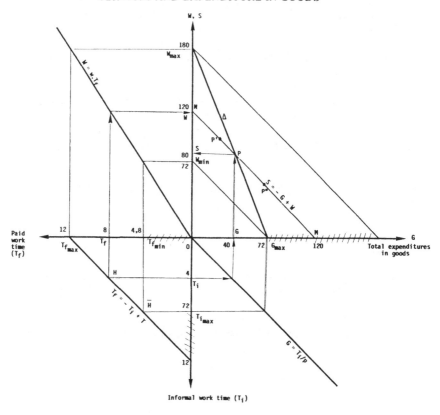

(The figures in the example : T = 12, w = 15, p = 1/10)

The set of points P meeting this condition is determined according to the
constraints

$$T_f : T - T_i$$

$$W = w . \ T_f = S + G \ \Bigg\} \Rightarrow \ S = - (w.p + 1) G + w.T,$$

$$G : T_i / p$$

This line is called the time-budget curve by Gershuny.

Following Gershuny, but at the same time rectifying the mistakes which
appeared in his formula [1983:28] we can state that:

$$S^* = \frac{w}{s} \ T - \frac{w.p.}{s} \ G^* \quad \text{where s and g are the prices, } S^* \text{ and } G^* \text{ the}$$

amount of services and goods respectively.

It can easily be verified (see Appendix 1) that, if the consumer can theoretically choose on the classical budget line MN a point which is different from P (for example P' or P" on Figure 2), it appears that he or she has no interest in these options, since any combination exterior to Δ corresponds to forced leisure and moves away from the ideal situation determined by the first optimisation.

Consequences for the optimal distribution

The constraint illustrated by the 'time-budget' line has two curious consequences that Gershuny has not noticed:

a) the domain of variation of H

- when the whole work period T is devoted to formal work (T_f $_{max}=T$), point H is situated on the X-axis ($T_{i\ min}=O$). At this point, the income is maximum ($W_{max}=w.T$) and is entirely devoted to the purchase of formal services ($S_{max}=W, G_{min}=0$) the point of consumption is located at the intersection of Δ with the Y-axis.

FIGURE 2

THE SYSTEM OF LINES OF INDIFFERENCE

(The figures in the example : s = 20, γ = 10, g = 2.4)

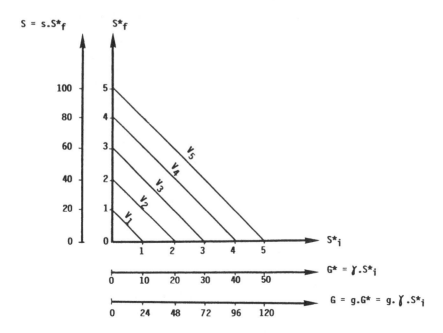

- when T_i increases, the point of consumption will move downwards: S decreases and G increases to reach a maximum at the point G_{max} of intersection of Δ with the X-axis ($S_{min} = O, G_{max} = \frac{w \cdot T}{wp+1}$)

This corresponds with a maximum of time devoted to informal work ($T_{i\ max} = \frac{w \cdot p \cdot T}{w \cdot p \cdot +1}$) and a minimum of time to paid work ($T_{f\ min} = T - T_{i\ max}$) (cf. point $\overline{H}$ of Figure 2).

Taking into account the productivity constraint of domestic work, T_i and T_f do not play a perfectly symmetrical part in the model since there exits a *lower limit* for T_f (which is not mentioned by Gershuny). Below this lower bound (curves b_1 and b_2 in his figure [1983:26]), the income is so low that the goods purchased by way of it (even if no formal service is consumed) do not permit the use of the whole potential T_i. Thus, there is some 'forced leisure' and a sub-optimal situation.

According to the assumptions of the model, it is never rational to work for the market a number of hours less than the limit. Therefore, there cannot be any total voluntary unemployment.

b) determination of the *optimum optimorum*
Beyond this stage, the second optimisation remains to be carried out. How does the household determine (in the limits given above) the distribution of its work time and thus the breakdown of its expenditures?

Surprising as it may seem, Gershuny does not directly tackle this issue. Hence, his model remains incomplete and, as we shall see later on, even contradictory.

Having explicitly assumed an indifference of the household between formal and informal work, the optimisation can only be carried out 'in the first quadrant', that is to say between goods (and so informal services) and formal services. This is where the contradiction in the model appears if we start with the assumption of a perfect substitution between formal and informal services, as Gershuny seems to do [assumption B2, 1983: 23] rather in the spirit of the model.

Let us elucidate this assumption: S* units of formal services provide the household with strictly the same satisfaction as S* units of domestic services. If the services are considered as perfectly divisible, the system of preferences can be constituted by a family of parallel lines (see Appendix 2) of equations:
$S_f^* = -S_i^* + V$ (where V is an utility index).
from which can be derived the system of preferences between expenditures on goods and expenditures on services:

$$S = s \cdot S_f^*$$
$$G = \gamma \cdot S_i^*$$
$$G = g \cdot G^* = \gamma \cdot g \cdot S_i^*$$

$\implies \quad S = -\frac{s}{g \cdot \gamma} \cdot G + V \cdot s$

(where γ is a constant coefficient of efficiency of goods in informal services)

Here too, we find a set of parallel lines of indifference. The optimisation leads to a noticeable result: two alternative 'corner' solutions:

case 1: the lines of indifference have a slope superior to that of   – the whole salary is spent on goods, the formal work time is minimal.
case 2: the slope of Δ is superior to that of the lines of indifference: the whole salary is spent in formal services, the time of formal work is at a maximum, and the informal work is nil.

It can also be noticed that when pushing the model to its extreme consequences it loses its power of prediction and contradicts the rest of the analysis. Does the approach lose its validity? We do not think so, provided we modify some basic assumption. *A priori,* four directions may be followed:

1. Giving up the assumption of absolute indifference by the households between formal and informal work.
2. Giving up the assumption of proportionality between consumed goods and produced informal services. In that case, the 'productivity' of the consumption of goods for the production of informal services (S_i^*/G^*) varies according to the amount of consumption. G is no longer proportional to S_i^* and the curves of indifference between S and G are no longer straight lines (even if we maintain the assumption of a perfect substitution between S_i^* and S_f^*). The optimum is found at the point of tangency between the line Δ with a curve V (G,S).
3. Abandoning the assumption of proportionality between goods consumed and necessary informal work. Here the 'productivity' of domestic work (measured by G^*/T_i^*) is no longer a constant, and the time-budget curve is no longer a straight line but a curve of which the point of tangency with an indifference curve determines the optimum.
4. By elaborating the parallel with the firm, a 'function of domestic production' could be conceived: $S_i^*=f(G^*,T_i^*)$. But, the two inputs being no longer complementary, the model would then lose the features which, according to Gershuny, provide it with its solidity and explicative power.

The assumptions of factual origin

The economic models are not mere logical constructions; they also refer to assumptions that are not resolved but considered sufficiently verified elsewhere to be included in this way of thinking.

The status of the two central assumptions in Gershuny's analysis are as follows:
a) the consumption of goods implies the use of (unpaid) work, whereas the consumption of formal services saves work.

b) the cost of domestic production decreases compared with the cost of services, owing to the faster growth of productivity in the manufacturing of goods, and to the free domestic work. For a similar final satisfaction, the domestic solution is cheaper. This accounts for the fact that it tends to be preferred.

But these two assumptions are far from being evident: On the one hand, the majority of formal services work not on the basis of an inert presence of the consumer with regard to the supplier, but according to a dynamic relation between the formal activity of the supplier and the informal activity of the consumer. The latter must be analysed as a component of the work time of the consumer, and not assimilated in free or leisure time. The time of education and training, of care, of applying to offices and civil services is no more fun or free than the time required for the daily journey (using transport services) from home to work. They are of a very diverse nature, but cannot be equalled to zero when domestic work is being evaluated. The new theory of consumption has had the advantage of stressing the constraints on domestic activity; it would theoretically be a backward step to exclude from these constraints those which correspond to the use of services. However, the general law of the comparative advantage in favour of domestic solutions and low improvements in productivity in services can also be contested. In this respect, we can verify [INSEE, 1984] that in France, between 1970 and 1982, public transport fares have increased more slowly than those of individual transport, that productivity in the French Railways has increased substantially and that the cost of travelling by train remains, according to the case, two or three times lower than the total cost of using a private vehicle.

In certain cases, similar technical procedures (though used at different levels) are at the origin of simultaneous improvements of productivity in the domestic sphere and formal services (laundry, microwave ovens, domestic cleaning). Finally, the services are likely to be organised and to accomplish economies of scale which should not, *a priori,* be overtaken by the improvements in the corresponding domestic technologies.

The conceptual framework

If this demonstration raises several questions of the internal coherence of the model, and if the major assumptions may, as we have just seen, be contested from the observation of practices of consumption, other elements of criticism concern the conceptual framework itself. They apply not only to Gershuny's model, but also to other contemporary models of consumer choice relying on the same basis.

The analysis is indeed hinged on two concepts whose apparent simplicity hides their limits: 'service-functions' and 'substitution'. The whole structure is based on the idea, taken from the new theory of final individual consumption, according to which human behaviour is related to universal categories of satisfaction or utility (service function). The only real problem is how these forms can be substantiated on the basis of alternative means is how these forms can be substantiated on the basis of alternative means (goods and services) in a formal or informal framework. Indeed, a close study of numerous service activities casts doubt on this postulate for the three following essential reasons:

1. A single technical function (for example, taking people from one place to another, eating and drinking, listening to music) generally covers social functions whose logic and growth factors are extremely different. The explanatory variables of eating out during the working day are not the same as those related to the evening meal or the meal at home: there is no substitution inside one single function, but competition between different functions, on the basis of distinct factors. To be effective, the basic unit of thinking should move from general technical functions to specific social functions.

2. 'Service-functions' are not fixed for ever; they change shape at the same time as their mode of production. New needs emerge that have no equivalent, even when they have antecedents, so that it is as vital to analyse the changes of the functions themselves as to envisage the likely substitutions that appear within them. How can we account for the emergence of new, more global needs, of social welfare, insuring against risks, professional training, communication and culture, inside fixed service-functions?

   The procedures based on the internal substitutability within pre-existing service functions seems to have a limited analytical score if the two previous remarks are accepted.

3. Even if precise functions could be isolated, there are no grounds for elevating the logic of substitution vis-à-vis the dynamics of complementarity between goods and services. This is evident as well in the coupling of goods and services within 'packages' which constitute new market products as in the constitution of production-consumption lines (ranging from production to supplying and to use, even to recycling) where the production of goods and services support each other without being substitutable. Moreover, this complementarity not only holds for goods and services, but also at times between self-services (as activities) and services, in so far as the practice of self-service is at the root of the development of new services – resorting to private vehicles leads to an increase in the services of driving schools, of automobile clubs, of training courses,and other services not related to goods (cars) but to the self-service activity itself.

More generally,the complexity of data to be processed in the domestic framework of self-service generates an increasing demand for services such as training, assistance and advice to households. Gershuny does mention some of these phenomena (using the notion of 'intermediary services') but does not draw the same conclusions as we do with regard to the limits of the theory of substitution.

THE SOCIAL MODEL OF SELF-SERVICE

The arguments of the preceding sections are based on the economic model and on the concepts used by Gershuny. But it would appear now that, in order to give an explanation of the results thus obtained, we must leave this analytical field and try to understand the historical and social context, that is to say, to carry out an analysis of the social model embedding this theory. This leads to isolating and questioning the major implicit social assumptions of Gershuny.

The Assumption Relative to the Family Model

By situating the basic unit of consumption practices at the level of the household rather than on the individual level, Gershuny is innovative and is enabled to link the external choices of the consuming units to their internal choices relative to domestic work. But this is achieved at the cost of the implicit invariance of the traditional familial model. Indeed, at the end of the analysis, Gershuny is led to conclude a probable reinforcement of this model in the future, since the increasing reliance on self-services is most likely to lead one member of the couple (probably female) to stop working and to carry out domestic tasks which become more and more productive as 'service-functions'.

Even if we remain cautious towards the correlated prospects of increasing female labour-market participation and the splitting-up of the traditional family, a minimum of statistical and sociological observation of the family leads to scepticism with regard to this first implicit social assumption. As things stand at present, the more developed economies (also from the point of view of Gershuny's model) are rather those where the traditional family loses more ground. Our aim is not to suggest an analysis of this phenomenon, but if it is acknowledged that the inversion of the trend in the female labour-market participation is not near at hand, we may think that it will be favourable neither to the nuclear familial model, nor to the decrease of the demand for formal services. The future of self-service would then be limited and would only be achieved by being shared in a more balanced way between males and females.

From this point of view, it would be of the utmost interest to elaborate, following for example, the research by Ingrosso in Italy [1984], typologies of families and households relating the demographic and social structure of these households to the forms and degrees of reliance on exterior services.

The Hypothesis of Social Homogeneity of Time

In the model under review, the initial distinction about time is that which opposes leisure time to total work time (formal and informal). Leisure time then seems empty – the analysis is based on the choices between formal and informal work, which constitute alternative means of obtaining final satisfaction.

However, on the one hand, it is well known that leisure time is in itself a period of time combining in its own way an activity, goods and services. On the other hand, its complement, the time for domestic work, is socially heterogeneous, ranging from highly constrained periods of time spent in repetitive tasks of the maintenance of goods and people, to periods of creativity close to leisure, or periods of time devoted to education and social relations whose growth might convey, according to Archambault [1985], a kind of 'tertiarisation' of domestic practices.[1]

Therefore, if time is structured as multidimensional time, we may wonder what must be retained from an analysis considering work time as a disutility, and opposing it, generally speaking, to leisure time – since certain periods spent on using goods (or resorting to services) are given a positive value; since do-it-yourself activities, bringing up children, or preparing meals are complex mixtures of constraints and pleasure; since paid work itself combines these dimensions of necessity and self-expression. Is it, therefore, not logical to substitute for the technical dichotomy of time allocation, a conceptual framework defining categories of periods of time associated to categories of social relations and constraints?

From such a point of view, another consequence would be to acknowledge that the diverse domestic or informal times are of a nature which is essentially different from the times of professional life and the times of recourse to formal services: They do not have the same value. Under these conditions the reluctance to be 'shut up' at home, leading to the growing exteriorisation of activity, or for others, awarding positive value to the return to (or staying at) home, will have an interpretation which differs from the traditional economic ones based on relative costs.

The Atomisation Hypothesis

The micro-economic approach of the consumption trends rests on an atomist approach of society. This initial characteristic is even more underlined by the conclusions of the analysis, which considers future society as an interconnected network of households consuming at home sounds, images and products of the new industry.

By definition, such a method, which elevates the *technical* inter-dependences between the agents, neglects the processes of *socialisation* of production, consumption and the relations between these two spheres.

There are numerous indicators of a sharp growth in the need for services which, before being backed by individual options, need to be inserted in more complex and more diverse social relations, including integration and participation of individuals in defining the general conditions of their existence, and insurance against individual or collective risks, professional or not.

Can this global need for 'services of socialisation' be analysed on the basis of micro-economic choices? If it is true that services like teaching and training are simultaneously techniques of transmission of knowledge and forms of experimentation or reproduction of social relationships, any analysis which considers only the first dimension proves to be powerless. And what are we to think of an approach to the growth of services insuring against professional or personal risks, or of consultancy services, in terms based on individual choices between goods and services?

CONCLUSION

Generally speaking, the omission of this social structure is the essential weak point in the theory of self-service. The more this theory provides stimulating tools of reflection on the minority of services which offer possibilities for substitution of domestic solutions and external services (subject to spotting truly comparable technical and social functions) the more it seems that, for most services, the social functions of the allegedly alternative options might be very far apart indeed, or, in other cases, that the intrinsically social nature of the needs excludes the use of purely micro-economic tools. We even assume that the theory of self-service provides the maximum of interest when the active participation of the consumer in the production of formal services of distribution, banking, education, leisure, etc., has to be studied, and not in the cases of substitution of goods and services in the final consumption.

Self-service would thus refer to a limited trend relying on factors both economic (relative costs) and non-economic which it would be appropriate to compare with the opposite trends to the socialisation of the activities, in order to grasp the tensions between these trends,and to understand the underlying challenges.

APPENDIX 1

Is point P an optimum?

With reference to Figure 1, the household can choose to consume fewer goods (to be located on segment NP),the fall in consumption $G' - G$ being offset by an increase in the expenditure in formal services: $S' = W - G' > S$ (Point P' of figure 1).

But as the use of informal work is proportional to the exenditure in goods, the time of real informal work is $T_{i_r} = p.G' < T_i$. The gap $(T_{i_e} = T_i - T_{i_r})$ represents 'forced leisure' and the total leisure is thus, under this assumption: $L + T_{i_e}$, which corresponds for the household to a sub-optimum situation.

The household can also decide to consume more goods (to be located on segment PM), the increase in consumption $(G'' - G)$ being offset by a decrease in the demand for formal service: $S'' = W - G'' < S$ (point P'' of figure 1). but the time of fixed informal work (T_i) no longer permits G'' to be absorbed. Two possibilities would then be offered to the households:

- limit itself to the length of domestic work T_i. But in that case, only the amount G of goods can be used: $(G''-G)$ would provide no satisfaction.
- lengthen the time of informal work from T_i to $T_{i''}(=p.G'')$, but in that case, the total time of work increases: $T''=T_f+T_i''>T$. Once again, we are in a sub-optimum situation. The line Δ is then the line of optimal points of distribution of expenditure when the distribution of T varies between formal and informal work.

APPENDIX 2

With reference to Figure 2 it can be noticed that a simple change of scale on the X-axis (S_i^*, $G^*= \gamma .S_i$, $G= \gamma .g.S_i^*$) and on the Y-axis (S_f^*, $S=s.S_f^*$) allows the change from the system of lines of indifference: V (S_i^*, S_f^*) to the system of indifference: $S=- \dfrac{s}{g \cdot \gamma} .G+V.s$, also composed of parallel lines (Figure 2).

NOTES

1. It may be noted, however, that a few years before the publication of J. Gershuny's books, anticipating papers on this theme had been written by J. Skolka in Austria [1976].
2. The sharp increase of these activities, in Europe as much as in the United States, is not compatible with the assumptions of self service.

REFERENCES

Archambault, E., 1985, 'Travail domestique et emploi tertiaire: substitution ou comp-lémentarité?' in M. Vernières (ed.), L'emploi du tertiaire, Paris: Economica.
Becker, G., 1965, 'A Theory of Allocation of Time', The Economic Journal, Vol. 30, No. 100.
Delaunay, J.C., and J. Gadrey 1987, 'Les enjeux de la société de service', Presses de la Fondation Nationale des Sciences Politiques, Paris.
Gadrey, J., 1986, 'Société de services ou de self-service)' Working Paper, Lille: Johns Hopkins European Center.
Gershuny, J., 1983, Social Innovations and the Division of Labour, Oxford: Oxford University Press.
Gronau, R., 1977, 'Leisure, Home Production and Work'; The Theory of Time Revisited', Journal of Political Economy, Vol. 85, No. 4.
Ingrosso, M., 1984, Strategie familiari e servizi sociali, Milan: F. Angeli.
INSEE, 1984, Les transports en France en 1981–82, Serie C115.
Linder, S., 1971 The Harried Leisure Class, New York: Columbia University Press.
Noyelle, T., 1983, 'The Rise of Advanced Services: Some Implications for Economic Development in U.S. Cities', Journal of American Planning Assocation, July.
Robbins, L., 1930, 'On the Elasticity of Demand for Income in Terms of Effort', Economica, June.
Skolka, J., 1976, 'Long-Term Effects of Unbalanced Labour Productivity Growth: On the Way to a Self-Service Society', in L. Solavi and J.R. de Pasqueri (eds.), Private and Enlarged Consumption, New York: North-Holland.
Stanback, T., 1979, Understanding the Service Economy, Baltimore: The Johns Hopkins University Press.

Only So Many Hours in a Day: Time Constraints, Labour Pools and Demand for Consumer Services

by

Hilary Silver

Some sociological sources of increasing demand for consumer services are discussed in this article. Contrary to J. Gershuny's theory of 'self-service', jobs in these industries are still growing, despite productivity improvements, due to increasing household demand generated by constraints placed on time by both paid and unpaid production and insufficient pools of household labour upon which to draw. Social trends with these effects include increasing female labour force participation and longevity, declining household size, later age at marriage, political struggles over state provision, and factors internal to the state itself.

INTRODUCTION

Consumer services have long been neglected in economic studies of industrial structure and change. Viewed as 'unproductive' or 'parasitic', they have been played down compared with the 'exportable' industries associated with goods. Yet, consumer services are receiving increased attention with the publication of three books by Jonathan Gershuny [1983, 1978 and Gershuny and Miles, 1983] outlining a new theory of these industries.[1] In contrast to most economic analyses, this work makes a major contribution by considering the inter-relationship of production and consumption, and by recognising the labour involved in the domestic economy. It builds on the 'new home economics' which uses micro-economic price theory to analyse the household as a firm maximising its utility with available resources.[2]

At the risk of oversimplifying an elegant and intricate theory, Gershuny's argument may be represented as a series of four propositions:

1. As household income rises, the demand for more luxurious service 'functions' or use-values also rises.
2. As household income rises, the marginal utility of income diminishes, changing the relative weights of income and substitution effects. The price of an additional hour of paid work declines, and its opportunity cost rises, relative to one spent in household labour or leisure. Thus, hours in paid work decline in

favour of time outside the labour force.
3. Because increasing productivity reduces the cost and increases the efficiency of consumer goods relative to final services, households satisfy their rising demand for service functions by substituting goods and 'self-service' for services.[3]
4. The aggregate effect of these household decisions is that demand for final consumer services – both marketed and non-marketed – should decline as households replace them with goods and their own labour in the informal economy. Employment in consumer services does not necessarily decline, however, due to lower productivity than in goods production.[4]

Drawing on data from the United States, this article considers some difficulties with this micro-economic model by examining the issues of time constraints and labour costs of self-service. Leaving aside the issue of the relative costs to households versus service firms of the material means of consumption, goods that are almost always more efficiently utilised by firms, it centres on sociological forces which may increase or reduce household time commitments with implications for the demand for consumer services.

TOWARDS A SOCIOLOGICAL EXPLANATION OF CONSUMER SERVICE DEMAND

Micro-economic models assume individuals (or households as units) face a scarcity of time allocated between paid and unpaid work and leisure (or consumption). Time constraints are reduced through social innovations that improve the productivity of goods and increase wages. This in turn reduces work time and/or enables the purchase of increasingly efficient consumer goods to reduce non-paid work time. In either case, 'free' time increases.

However, increasing quantities of consumer goods do not necessarily free one's total time, only its distribution among different activities. The value of an individual's total time is a function not only of his/her rate of pay and hours of work, but also the uses to which time must be allocated to an expanding array of consumption activities, not only unpaid work. Deriving indirect utility (work) cannot be substituted for direct utility (leisure) indefinitely; people must still eat and sleep. The marginal utility of leisure then is a function of the extent of total 'constrained time' [Preteceille and Terrail, 1985]; or hours committed to producing for a wage and for consumption. More goods, regardless of their productivity, simply tie up more time in using and maintaining them.[6] This produces the 'harriedness' of daily life among even wealthy families [Linder, 1970].

The decision to serve oneself – to expend one's own labour with or without goods – instead of being served for any given use is thus a function of the value of leisure to the consumer, not just of the hours of work at the market wage and the relative price of goods to services. At high incomes, the budget constraint is overwhelmed by time constraints. The only way to enjoy a wider range of use-values and to increase one's standard of living is to turn to the time of others.

Moreover, some uses, physiological needs aside, are not amenable to goods. As Hirschmann [1973] has shown, 'man does not live by consumption alone'. Striving for power, prestige, respect and love, friendships, politics and pursuit of truth and salvation, are income-elastic, so that even high-earners may become overcommitted through time over-runs of these activities. These 'obituary-improving' tasks, which often bestow greater utility than obsessive goods consumption, enmesh individuals in the time constraints of others and may promote a common formal solution (e.g. clubs, organisations, parties, churches, maybe even marriage).

Although some economists of time recognise that consumption and non-economic behaviour have durations,they have not considered the social relations of consumption – the ability or inability to pool or redistribute consumption-related labour – which may influence both an individual's and the social stock of time. To indicate how this works, I adopt Gershuny's micro-economic rhetoric to draw macro-economic conclusions about service industries from rational individual behaviour.

People can free time committed to social and cultural life, consumption, and unpaid work with access to the labour and time of others. This can be obtained from either paid or unpaid sources. The unpaid sources are in the household or socialised labour pool; the paid source is in purchased consumer services. For those with higher incomes, where only a time constraint is effective, demand for final consumer services will rise; for those with lower incomes, who are subject to budget constraints as well, access to others' labour may be obtained by non-market means. The demand for certain consumer services reflects the aggregate economic or political efforts of consumers, particularly those under greater time constraints or without access to household labour pools, to externalise and socialise the costs of time committed to unpaid labour. Socialisation or collective consumption is often, although not always, more productive than having the consumer expend his/her own labour.[7]

Of course, not all consumer services save time. A useful distinction can be made between time-conserving and time-expensive services. The output of some services is a transformation of the consumer which requires him/her to be present for the duration of the producer's labour activity. To consume, or derive utility from, medical care, education, a restaurant meal, or a haircut may appear to be as costly in time as self-service. Nevertheless, what is saved is not only energy but also the time that would have had to be committed to acquiring medical, academic, cooking or barbering skill personally instead of relying on the social division of labour. Thus, time-expensive services which rely on specialised skills none the less indirectly save time over the consumer's life-cycle.[8]

Time-conserving services, in contrast, usually consist of labour otherwise devoted to operating, maintaining or improving objects other than the consumer. Vacuuming, car maintenance or,at the extreme, caring for children or the aged are all time-consuming unpaid work commitments that can be eliminated or reduced by purchasing or gaining access to the labour of others.

These services are the focus of the rest of this article, which indicates some of the sociological trends, especially in household structure and politics, responsible for increasing the demand for these time-saving final consumer services. While Gershuny's model implies increasing amounts of free time, my model considers a variety of economic and social forces that raise the amount of time tied up in paid and unpaid work and reduce the access to others' labour. As a consequence, demand is generated for the labour and time of others, commodified as consumer services. When that labour can be purchased directly, employment in marketed services is generated; when it is provided as a consequence of political struggles, socialised non-marketed services grow.

TRENDS INCREASING THE DEMAND FOR CONSUMER SERVICES

Several sociological trends have increased the amount of time households have committed to some form of labour – be it for consumption or production – and have contributed to the rising demand for consumer services in recent years. This is by no means an exhaustive list; it is meant to be indicative of the non-economic factors to be considered in analysing these industries. US government data are used throughout.

Increasing Female Labour Force Participation

The tasks of household production changed considerably over the past century as a vast array of goods and services were commodified and produced socially by wage labour. The increasing demand for female wage workers has brought growing numbers into the labour force, restricting the total time and labour available in married couple households.

As income increased with industrialisation during the nineteenth century, most working women were concentrated in private household work where they 'trained' in housework tasks before marriage and were sheltered from work deemed unrespectable by the 'Cult of Domesticity.' Although a minority of women did obtain early factory jobs, particularly those associated with their traditional role of garment-making, these opportunities were limited over time by male unions and restrictive labour legislation. However, by the turn of the century, as the service sector expanded, many tasks performed by women in their own households were commodified and typed as 'women's work.' Native white working women moved into these so-called clean, respectable clerical and retail jobs, as well as positions requiring formal education, such as teaching and nursing. Domestic service was left to predominantly black and immigrant women excluded from the expanding sectors.

Thus, female labour force participation in America began to rise early in the twentieth century, first among single females, then among married mothers. By 1940, 48 .1 per cent of single women, 14.7 per cent of married women with a husband present, and 32 per cent of widowed or divorced women were in the labour force. A shortage of young workers from 1945 until the 1960s helped bring women of all marital statuses into the labour force in greater numbers than ever before, even as fertility was rising. By 1985, 65.2 per cent of single women, 54.2 per cent of married childless women, and 42.8 per cent of widows and divorcees were working. Overall, female labour force participation, using all adult women as a base,rose from 27.4 per cent to today's 54.5 per cent [US Bureau of the Census, 1986: 398]. Using women 65 years of age and under as a base, 64 per cent of all women were in the labour force in 1986 [Bergmann, 1986:21].

Oppenheimer [1970] has persuasively argued that labour demand in the service industries, rather than supply-side factors, is responsible for rising female labour force participation. This is reflected in the continuous rise of women's wages over the century which increased the opportunity costs of staying at home.[9] At the same time, male wages also rose, indicating that women did not displace men from their own jobs. The long-term decline in male participation was due primarily to earlier retirements, not competition from women. Indeed, the rising demand for labour directed the sexes into non-competing labour markets, with women dispro-portionately recruited for service sector jobs. Women's employment segregation was also associated with lower pay for their jobs. Throughout the twentieth century, women's wages remained about 60 per cent of men's, making them a cheap source of badly needed educated labour which further increased female labour force participation.

Table 1 indicates how employment grew precisely in the service industries labelled as 'women's work'.[10] It also shows how women's employment segregation persisted despite their changing distribution among industries over time. Women have been much more likely to work in the service sector than men and have thus benefited from the increasing demand for workers in these industries. The data also indicate that in every year since 1910, women were concentrated in different industries than men. Women were always under-represented in extractive industries, but like men, left these jobs over the century. They were also under-represented in transformative work, but like men, increased their involvement until 1950. After that, women left these industries earlier than men. Women remain slightly less likely to work in distributive services then men, although the gap has narrowed as the retail trade component of this sector expanded. Over time, as clerical work has grown, women have increased their representation in producer services so that today they hold an edge in these industries.

Where women have always been substantially over-represented is in the consumer services. As social services increased, so did women's disproportionate share of these jobs. Today, one-third of all working women are in this sector. Similarly, as personal services substantially declined since 1910, female over-representation in these industries has

TABLE 1

Employed Americans[1]

Sector[5]	1910	1930	1940	1950	1960	1970	1980	1985
Extractive[4]	.36	.24	.21	.14	.08	.04	.04	.04
Transformative	.28	.29	.29	.33	.34	.33	.30	.27
Distributive	.18	.21	.20	.22	.21	.22	.21	.21
Producer	.07	.13	.05	.05	.06	.08	.11	.12
Social[2] ⎫	.10	.10	.10	.12	.16	.22	.25	.23
Personal[3] ⎭			.14	.12	.11	.10	.10	.12

Employed Women

Sector[5]	1910	1930	1940	1950	1960	1970	1980	1985
Extractive[4]	.22	.09	.04	.04	.02	.01	.02	.02
Transformative	.25	.22	.22	.24	.22	.21	.19	.16
Distributive	.10	.16	.17	.21	.19	.20	.20	.19
Producer	.12	.21	.05	.06	.08	.10	.13	.15
Social[2] ⎫	.32	.29	.19	.21	.25	.33	.35	.33
Personal[3] ⎭			.31	.22	.19	.15	.13	.15

Sources: US Bureau of the Census, 1914, *Thirteenth Census of the United States: Population (1910),* Vol IV: Occupation Statistics, Washington, Government Printing Office; 1932, *Fifteenth Census of the United States: Population,* Vol III, Part I, Washington, GPO; 1943, *Sixteenth Census of the United States: 1940 – Population,* Vol. III: The Labor Force, Part I: U.S. Summary, Washington, GPO, Table 74; 1955, *United States Census of Population 1950,* Vol. IV: Special Reports, Part I, Chapter D: Industrial Characteristics, Washington, GPO, Table 1; 1963, *United States Census of Population 1960,* PC(2)-7C Subject Reports: Occupation by Industry, Washington, GPO, Table 2; 1973, *1970 Census of Population,* PC(2)-7B Subject Reports: Industrial Characteristics, Washington, GPO, Table 1; 1984, *1980 Census of Population,* PC80-1-D1-A, Detailed Population Characteristics, Part I, Section A: US Summary, Washington, GPO, Table 285; US Department of Labor, Bureau of Labor Statistics, 1986, *Employment and Earnings,* Vol. 33, No. 12, January.

Notes: 1. Refers to gainful workers 10 years or over in 1910 and 1930; employed workers 14 years or older 1940–60; and employed workers 16 years or older after that.
2. Social and personal services overlap in 1910 and 1920.
3. Excludes entertainment in 1910 and 1930.
4. Farm workers, especially women as unpaid family workers, may have been overcounted in 1910 when special attention was give to the female labour force; they may be undercounted in 1920, throwing off the entire distribution.
5. Comparability before 1940 is imprecise because the industry classification was limited until then. See note 10.

fallen as well. While a third of all working women held jobs in this category in 1910 (compared with 10 per cent of the entire labour force), only 15 per cent of them did in 1980 (compared with 12 per cent of all employed workers). In sum, while women have a different sectoral distribution than men, they have become less segregated in personal services and more so in social services over time.

As women entered the labour force to fill the expanding consumer services, their time commitments to work – both paid and unpaid –

increased considerably. This is reflected in the fact that working women reduce the number of hours they devote to housework. Comparing time use surveys taken in 1967–68 and 1975–76 is methodologically hazardous, but it does appear that wives, whether employed or not, have lowered their contributions to housework over time. For non-working wives, this may be due to more productive consumer goods and may reflect increasing free time. But for wives who enter full-time work, their housework precipitously declines by more than 30 hours a week [Bergmann, 1986: 264–5].

Gershuny's theory thus receives some support among full-time housewives, who increase their household's labour pool, although even their leisure varies considerable over the life cycle [Deem, 1986]. But for the increasing proportion of working wives, the theory is less tenable. First, Gershuny argues that these women's time commitments in the home and diminishing marginal utility for income cause them to reduce their paid labour time or take part-time jobs to begin with.[11] There is little empirical support for this notion. For one thing, since the 1960s, surveys have found that, given a choice among working the same, fewer, or more hours at the same wage rate, workers dissatisfied with their hours choose to work longer four times more often than those preferring to work less. Indeed, in 1985 for prime-age men, the substitution effect far outweighed the income effect, so that the backward-bending supply curve was not observed. Even among women in the childbearing years, the group most likely to express a desire to trade leisure for income, only ten per cent preferred to work fewer hours. Examined by industry, only 20 per cent of workers in public administration wanted to work more hours, compared with 40 per cent of those in retail trade, which has a high proportion of part-time workers who are apparently in such positions involuntarily [Katona, et al., 1971: 128–33; Best, 1978; Shank, 1986: 40–44].

Furthermore, the inverse relation between husband's and wife's incomes, which used to indicate a trade-off between paid and unpaid work, has disappeared over time, implying that families continue to prefer more income to buy new commodities. Statistics also show that lower-wage workers work fewer hours overtime than higher-wage workers, whose marginal utility for income should be lower [Sharp, 1981: 135]. Institutional constraints, from union rules to legal hours and retirement ages, have more to do with declines in work time than voluntary supply decisions. Part-time work appears to be more an employers' strategy to reduce labour costs than workers' strategy to clear time for consumption labour. Part-time women earn 25 per cent less an hour than full-time, ignoring the loss of fringe benefits, and are even more concentrated in low-paid occupations than women as a whole [Smith, 1979]. In fact, as a proportion of all workers, part-timers are no longer increasing (see Table 2).

American women clearly did not increase their labour force participation over the past 20 years by taking mostly part-time jobs. The proportion of women working full-time held fairly steady, at about 75 per cent, throughout the entire period. Nearly half the women with any labour market involvement now work full-time all year [Flaim, 1986]. In fact 71

TABLE 2

RATIO OF VOLUNTARY PART-TIME TO FULL-TIME WORKERS

	1965	1970	1975	1979	1980	1981	1982	1983
All Workers	.13	.16	.17	.16	.17	.17	.17	.16
Women Workers	.24	.27	.27	.26	.26	.26	.26	.25

Source: US Bureau of Labor Statistics, *Handbook of Labor Statistics,* Bulletin 2217 (June 1985), Table 7.

per cent of mothers with jobs worked full-time in 1985; even 67 per cent of mothers with children under three did so [Bergmann, 1986: 24].

If reducing paid work is being resisted, another alternative is to reduce the time committed to domestic labour. However, Gershuny's suggestion of acquiring more and more productive consumer goods is not, as I have argued, a solution. First, the proliferation of labour-saving devices has not promoted increasing female labour-force participation in the past, which suggests that such goods do not free time.[12] Second, since consumption itself takes time, the acquisition of more goods commits consumers to longer hours by broadening their range of tasks. As income rises and there is more to consume, every additional purchase means an additional demand on time and energy in order to consume (and maintain) it, creating an opportunity cost of not being able to consume what is already possessed. This multiplies instead of alleviates the constraints on time.

Labour Pools, Fertility and Child Care

Another solution might be to reduce commitments specifically to those tasks which are most time-consuming and for which there are few substitutable goods. For example, children are particularly demanding of time and so women may decide to limit their fertility. Indeed, there has been a secular decline in childbearing, although, unlike female labour force participation which kept rising throughout the century, fertility increased temporarily between 1946 and the early 1960s. Although no one theory has accounted entirely for the 'baby boom' anomaly, it has been explained as an interaction between female employment, the female wage rate, and fertility. In general, higher male incomes increase fertility while higher female incomes, which increase female employment, reduce it. During the 1950s not enough women were yet employed to be price-sensitive to female wage rates and so the income effects of husband's wage predominated. But over time it appears that the effect of female wages has offset that of men, reducing fertility. As more and more women took jobs, the opportunity costs in income of not working in the formal economy rose and in turn, fertility declined. This trend is also encouraged by the increasing cost of investing in children's human capital. More resources are invested per child, raising the opportunity costs of unpaid work and encouraging smaller families. Households trade off quantity for the quality of and income invested in their children (England, 1986:77–83).

Nevertheless, even one child enormously increases the time constraints on parents. Are there any other alternatives? Women might try to increase their access to the labour of others, to pool the household's labour resources, redistribute them, and even achieve some economies of scale. Indeed, patriarchal gender relations have long enabled men to increase leisure through their access to labour of others in the household. While there is some indication that men have slightly increased the hours they spend in domestic labour,[13] the time husbands devote to housework remains a small fraction of that spent by wives.

Why do husbands not increase their share of housework, if they now have the labour-saving devices Gershuny expects them to enjoy? The new home economics and exchange theories which treat families as utility maximising units cannot explain this, since male housework is unrelated to the relative wage rates of husbands and wives. Even when wives earn more or work longer than their husbands, men do not increase their contribution to the domestic economy. Nor do they do so when they hold more egalitarian sex role attitudes. Only the presence, number and age of children, or a wife working the nightshift, appears to increase male housework. Child care is immediate and demanding. Such situational factors restrict male access to the household labour pool to meet these demands on time, men may contribute marginally more to household chores (England 1986:94–9).

If the ability of women to dip into the household labour pool is limited by non-economic behaviour, there are two other avenues to the labour of others to lighten the burden of domestic labour: either buy other people's time or force them, through the state, to share it. Both approaches generate demand for consumer services produced in the formal economy.

Consider child care. Unquestionably, the preference of women to work more hours is related to availability of child care services. Mothers with children under five years old are the least likely to participate in the labour force. Fully 24 per cent of full-time working women in these circumstances and 12 per cent of part-timers would work more hours if child care were available (Presser and Baldwin, 1980:1202–6). Thus, there is considerable pent-up demand for 'consumer services' of this nature. The vast bulk of child care services continues to be produced in the informal economy – either in the child's own household or in another's, whether a relative's or non-relative's. Only a small percentage participate in socialised care programmes such as nurseries, day care centres, and the like, but this category is the fastest growing of all. Around 1960, less than 200,000 spaces were available in licensed day care centres in America; by 1972, there were 1,021,202, evenly split between non-profit and for-profit agencies [US Department of Labor, 1975:35].

While household provision of child care still predominates, Table 3 offers further evidence that the demand for socialised child care has exploded with increased female labour force participation. The trends indicate that whatever the growth in the informal economy for other activities, child care is increasingly becoming commodified. Today, at least 79 per cent of full-time employed mothers pay some cash for child care, even to their relatives.

A similar labour-pooling, time-saving logic explains why eating and drinking places are among the fastest growing industries of the post-war era. Between 1952 and 1982, US restaurant sales, corrected for inflation, rose 220 per cent, compared with a growth of 160 per cent in total consumer expenditures over that period [Bergman, 1986: 280]. Not only have restaurants specialised by cuisine and diversified enormously in line with consumer tastes, but fast-food chains have also increased productivity considerably. Today the 'take-away' business is growing even faster than McDonalds'-style restaurants.

To sum up the discussion so far, female labour force participation and patriarchal structuring of household labour impose time constraints on working women, especially working mothers, whose increased earnings generate demand for more time-conserving social and consumer services.

Other Demographic Changes: Longevity and Smaller Households

Gershuny's analysis assumes a conventional household in which at least two people pool their labour. But if married women have trouble freeing

TABLE 3

CHILD CARE ARRANGEMENTS 1958–82

Mothers Employed Full-Time	1982	1977	1965	1958
	(children under 5)		(children under 6)	
Care in child's home	27.2	28.6	47.2	56.6
by relative	21.8	22.0	28.7	42.4
by non-relative	5.4	6.6	18.5	14.2
Care in other's home	46.3	47.4	37.3	27.1
by relative	20.8	20.8	17.6	14.5
by non-relative	25.5	26.6	19.6	12.7
Child care centre	19.9	14.6	8.2	4.5
Other	6.9	9.3	7.4	11.8
Mothers Employed Part-time				
Care in child's home	41.2	42.7	47.0	
by relative	34.6	34.3	38.5	
by non-relative	6.6	8.4	8.6	
Care in other's home	35.7	28.8	17.0	
by relative	16.4	13.2	9.1	
by non-relative	19.3	15.6	7.9	
Child care centre	7.9	9.1	2.7	
Other	15.2	19.4	33.2	

Sources: US Bureau of the Census, 1982, *Trends in Child Care Arrangements of Working Mothers,* Current Population Reports, P–23, no. 117, Washington, GPO, p.6 and 1983, *Child Care Arrangements of Working Mothers: June 1982,* CPR P–23, no.129, Washington, GPO, p.4.

TABLE 4

DEMOGRAPHIC TRENDS

	1910	1930	1940	1950	1960	1970	1980	1984	r1	r2
Female Labour										
Force Participation[1]	.22	.25	.30	.36	.42	.50	.60	.64	.91	−.98
% L.F. Female	.19	.22	.25	.29	.33	.38	.42	.44	.94	−.96
Women's Earnings[2]	70	100	140	180	220	240	250	255	.95	−.91
Fertility[3]	3.5	2.3	2.1	3.0	3.5	1.9	1.7	1.8	−.90	.80
% Female-Headed										
Households			.11	.09	.10	.11	.15	.16	.78	−.94
% Family Households			.92	.89	.85	.81	.74	.73	−.90	.96

r1 = Pearson correlation with % working women in social services 1950–84 (N = 5)
r2 = Pearson correlation with % working women in personal services 1950–84 (N = 5)

Notes: 1.   Labour force participation of women 65 years old or less. Last figure is for March
1986.
2.   Weekly earnings of women workers in 1984 dollars.
3.   Births per white woman of childbearing age. Last figure is for 1982.

Sources: Barbara Bergmann, 1986, *The Economic Emergence of Women,* New York, Basic,
pp.20–21, 26, 42; US Bureau of the Census, 1986, *Statistical Abstract of the United
States 1986* and 1970, *Historical Statistics of the United States,* Washington, GPO.

their time by increasing their access to other people's labour except through
marketed or state services, households with only one adult enjoy even fewer
benefits from family labour pooling. The number of such households have
mushroomed.[14]

In 1960, only 7 per cent of American families with children were
maintained by women without husbands present. In 1984, 23 per cent of
families were female-headed [Bergmann, 1986: 229]. Since many of these
households are poor, they cannot increase their access to additional labour
by purchasing it; instead, they rely on non-profit social services which
expand in response.

Postponing marriage also increased the proportion of households
containing a single person. Indeed, marriage and childbirth later in life may
actually be economically rational in that it conserves time and income that
would otherwise be committed to non-working family members. Surveys
show that single people and young families without children are most likely
to purchase services of all kinds on the market rather than perform 'self-
service' in their homes [Bergmann, 1986]. One reason for this is the absence
of additional labour – a 'wife' – to perform domestic tasks and the absence
of children to make demands on time and income. For those young single
people who can afford it, the market offers one source of assistance.
Indeed, many have commented on the consumption styles of young urban
professionals.

Increasing longevity also adds to the number of childless and single
households. Small older households are particularly dependent on access
to assistance from others as their productivity at 'self-service' declines.
Thus, an ageing population generates new demand for medical insurance,
specialised transport and recreation services, as well as government

employment to administer social security pensions.

All of these demographic changes reduce the size of households and thereby constrict the informal labour pool upon which individuals may draw. The result: increasing demand for marketed and state services. When the market does not respond to it, politicians often do.

Political Struggles over Consumption

Until now, the ways in which the state indirectly influences the growth of consumer services have been left implicit. Government policies can inhibit or encourage female labour force participation (through family, labour, and child care laws) as well as household size (through welfare, medical, and divorce policies). But the state also directly generates employment in consumer services. To see this, it is necessary to consider why some services are performed by the state rather than the market. Some domestic tasks are particularly inefficient when performed in each and every individual household. They include tasks which require very expensive capital equipment (e.g., roads), or specialised skills (e.g., medical knowledge), or considerable power over others (e.g., co-ordinating individual activities). Clearly in these cases, socialising labour (and the goods to work with) would be more efficient [Archambault, 1985]. However, it may not be profitable. In cases where the risks of investment are high or the capital needed is immense, the private sector is unlikely to provide the service. Indeed, whenever it can produce a service profitably, it tends to do so in competition with the state, e.g., private medicine. The political struggles over the 'privatisation' of both state capital and welfare services reflect the possibility of for-profit alternatives.

If the market is unresponsive, the 'non-sovereign consumer' faces a dilemma. It is patently inefficient, given time and resource limitations, for each household to try to acquire all specialised skills or consumer goods, or to regulate and co-ordinate all social relations only for its own members. Yet, an alternative means of co-ordinating and socialising the collective needs of all households may develop. In some cases, a social movement (e.g., for needs regarding the natural environment), in others, a political party, especially working-class or popular-based parties, try to influence the state to use its power to increase consumption of these services through socialised provision. Thus, the growth of social services reflects political relations more than economic ones. Yet, political struggles over consumption can be seen to derive, at the level of households as least, from the same mechanisms of constrained time.

In fact, the state has always played a major role in structuring the time available for paid and domestic labour, as well as leisure. While employers have always sought to structure workers' time into captive (wage-labour) and free (unpaid) time, the state has played an important role in structuring the time of workers not only as wage-labour but as consumers as well [Duclos, 1981]. On the one hand, regulation of hours uniformly shortened the working day and week, but then the bureaucratic provision of public services was limited to school, clinic or office hours, creating scheduling conflicts between production and consumption obligations. Now state policies attempt to stagger work hours through flexitime, shiftwork, and work-sharing. They are also trying to influence the scheduling of holidays to avoid crowding and environmental deterioration. Blue laws kept workers from working or consuming services from the formal economy at weekends; with their repeal, one-quarter of all American workers work on Saturday and one eighth on Sunday. One sixth of full-time workers and half of part-time workers work outside typical daylight hours, usually in the evening. Nevertheless, only 12 per cent of American workers enjoy flexitime or other variable work schedules; socialised production often requires workers to be on the job at the same time [*Monthly Labor Review*, November, 1986]. One irony is that as the state socialised consumption and intervened in work hours, it freed time for workers to devote to further political struggles. In this way, social services may increase further.

In addition to political demands by consumer-citizens, however, the state itself may generate employment growth in non-marketed services for its own reasons. Defence and war-making,and the maintenance of a standing army and police force may be economically wasteful, but create jobs in response to the logic of power. Similarly, Urry [1987] has argued that bureaucrats and professionals, as members of a 'service class', may use their occupational clout to enhance their numbers for reasons of prestige and power.

This political analysis of non-marketed services again contrasts with Gershuny's, which considers only the relative costs of collective versus domestic informal provision. Productivity in the state sector lags, it is argued, because of the lack of market competition. The state, as a monopoly, avoids pressure to improve the quality or efficiency of service provision, and can command its own price, expressed in taxes. This provokes ubiquitous tax revolts and underground, tax-evading informal service provision. The proposed solution is to reduce the cost of government services by increasing the contribution of communal labour.

This is a surprising conclusion from a theory advocating the hyper-consumption of personal goods in the privacy of one's own home. The drive for personal goods acquisition implied by such individualised consumption tends to erode public life rather than promote communal consumption in clubs, pubs, and so on. Moreover, after proposing a transfer of labour costs from government to communities in order to reduce taxes, Gershuny's rationale for advocating government construction of new high-tech infrastructures, transferring huge costs from goods producers to taxpayers, remains unclarified. Even if the latter were more economically productive, it might not be more politically expedient in forestalling tax revolts.

IMPLICATIONS FOR EMPLOYMENT IN CONSUMER SERVICES

If demand for consumer services rises, what are the implications for employment? Gershuny views proportional expansion of jobs in the consumer services as a reflection of their relatively low productivity. However, employment in these industries is not only growing relative to labour-shedding manufacturing, but also in absolute terms (see Table 5). The only way this could occur, together with the falling demand for final services that Gershuny proposes, would be for these industries to have negative productivity gains, which is unlikely.

In contrast, this article has analysed these services as a means of buying time, i.e. other people's labour, to substitute for the consumer's. By their very nature,and regardless of the goods used, consumer services tend to be labour-intensive. Thus, as demand rises, so too should employment in these industries. Indeed, a case can be made that demand for these services is so great that employment grows despite productivity *gains* in their delivery [Fisk, 1985; Herman, 1986; Brand and Ahmed, 1986].

TABLE 5

SECTORAL EMPLOYMENT 1970-1985

SECTOR	*1970*	*1980*	*1985*
EXTRACTIVE	3,440,693	3,941,767	4,277,000
TRANSFORMATIVE	25,492,955	29,026,978	29,352,000
DISTRIBUTIVE	17,041,770	20,746,584	22,386,000
PRODUCER	6,372,896	10,336, 829	13,281,000
SOCIAL	16,638,716	23,936,010	25,008,000
medical	4,430,962	7,250,465	7,910,000
education	6,354,430	8,377,213	8,254,000
non-profit	1,339,819	2,178,324	2,217,000
postal	745,311	720,899	728,000
government	3,590,016	5,147,466	4,995,000
misc. social	178,178	261,643	904,000
PERSONAL	7,566,131	9,621,189	12,845,000
private household	1,252,445	701,460	1,254,000
hotels	737,600	1,051,811	1,451,0000
eating/drinking	2,465,690	4,181,272	5,244,000
repair	1,001,646	1,357,081	1,971,000
laundries	588,709	399,862	415,000
barbers/beauty	713,367	665,678	805,000
entertainment	631,789	1,007,070	1,278,000
misc. personal	175,885	257,055	427,000
TOTAL LABOUR FORCE	76,553,599	97,639,355	107,150,000

Sources: See Table 1.

Tables 1 and 5 present employment shifts among industrial sectors, classified into categories developed by Joachim Singelmann [1978].[15] Only two US industries registered declines in employment since 1980: education and public administration. Decline in the first was due to falling enrolments as the 'baby bust' replaced the 'baby boom' generation. Decline in government was due to politics: the election of the conservative Reagan administration. Whether these cutbacks will continue, however, is an open question. Indeed, public administration did not suffer as much employment loss as some had expected because state and local government took over some of the federal services that were cut.

In contrast, the decline in personal services has levelled off and recently, this sector has rebounded.[16] An examination of specific industries reveals an association between these increases and the 'industrialisation of housework', in support of the argument presented. Private households, barber/beauty shops and laundries, after decades of job loss, actually increased in employment during the early 1980s. Employment in eating and drinking establishments continues to expand, as well as in paid child care (Table 3). There has also been growth in repair services to maintian investments in domestic capital.

Demographic changes, especially ageing, also appear to have been important. With the growing retired population, recreation and entertainment services, as well as hotels, increased. Nor were marketed personal services the only ones to grow; the strongest expansion of consumer services was in social services, particularly those related to health. Jobs in medical services almost doubled since 1970.

Nor are consumer services expected to shrink over the next decade. On the contrary, the Bureau of Labor Statistics [1984] estimates that of the 14 million new jobs in services expected between 1984 and 1995, 1.2 million will be in eating and drinking places, 2.8 million in retailing, 0.3 million in the non-profit sector, 0.2 million in entertainment, and 1.9 million in health. Indeed, the *only* personal or social services projected to lose employment between 1982 and 1995 are private households. Even government, despite its recent job decline and rising productivity since 1967, is expected to grow [see Personick, 1985; Silver, Delaunay and Gadrey, 1986; Fisk, 1985].

Thus, consumer services in America have expanded, and will continue to do so in the foreseeable future. As Table 1 indicates, 35 per cent of total employment was in the combined social and personal services during the 1980s, compared with 24 per cent in 1940. While most of the spectacular growth in social services occurred during the 1960s boom, these industries with few exceptions continue to grow, some quite rapidly. Personal services are now adding jobs faster than at any time in the past half-century. And all this is occurring despite productivity increases.

CONCLUSION

This article has argued that non-economically motivated behaviour and a number of social trends have played a role in generating greater demand for, and employment in final consumer services. Time spent in paid work is not voluntarily declining, and social changes, such as female labour force participation and shrinking household size, have increased constraints on time and reduced access to pools of labour and time in households. Since widespread ownership of goods does not free time, but rather adds new commitments, and since an expanded array of consumption activities itself takes time, self-service with personal property is not a solution. Rather, harried people seek someone else to devote time to using and maintaining the goods, or developing the skills that are necessary inputs to consumption. If time is more valuable than income, marketed consumer services are purchased; if it is not, political pressure builds for collective provision. Employment trends indicate that personal services, particularly those that conserve working women's time commitments to household labour or extend time by prolonging life itself, have grown apace.

This is not to deny that the sociological trends increasing demand for consumer services may themselves be determined by economic change. On the contrary, it was shown that female labour force participation is caused by increasing demand for consumer services. While women's wages have risen, bringing more of them into paid work, the gap between their and men's wages continues to keep services affordable. Similarly, the need for more productive workers, it can be argued, increases demand for services enhancing human capital. Indeed, the rhetoric of economically motivated behaviour was adopted in this article to indicate the power of micro-economic reasoning in explaining macro-economic trends.

Nor is the argument meant to diminish Gershuny's valuable contribution in calling attention to the inter-relationship of social institutions and the myth of separate spheres so often found in economic and sociological writing. Modern social science has inherited from the classics, perhaps from liberalism itself, a tendency to treat the differentiation of public and private, workplace and residence, economy and family as absolute rather than as a tendency. Post-war theories present the specialisation of the household in 'expressive' tasks as a *fait accompli* [Parsons 1949, 1955], building theories of the family on the premise that it is devoid of all but consumption activities, providing a refuge from the emotional and physical ravages of work in the capitalist economy [Zaretsky, 1976]. This assumption is as true of the 'embourgeoisement' theorists as it is of those who see it as a source of potentially revolutionary human development. Sociologists have mistakenly presumed that the household is exclusively a sphere of leisure, self-expression, reproduction and consumption rather than as one of work.

The recent contribution of the new home economics school as well as of feminist scholars is the recognition that production continues to take place in the home, as an aspect of consumption. Theories of the informal and underground economy, such as Gershuny's, call attention to household production for the market as well. However, Gershuny's theory remains incomplete. The 'de-differentiation' of economy and household is attributed only to social innovation and its attendant productivity advantages. Such economic models neglect the importance of gender, political and other social relations, social inter-dependence and the ability to pool time and labour, and changing relationships among social institutions in determining the development of consumer services.

NOTES

The author is grateful to Jean Gadrey and Jonathan Gershuny for their comments.

1. The discussion centres on Gershuny [1983].
2. The household's relationship with the economy is through outputs, such as sustenance, health, emotional soundness, and socialised children, and inputs, such as marketed goods and services. Decisions about the number of children to have or the division of paid and unpaid labour between the sexes are made rationally, within the constraints of prices, incomes and time [Becker, 1981; Schultz, 1981, 1974; Linder, 1970; Lancaster, 1966; Evans, 1972; Sharp, 1981].
3. In contrast to seeing an inverse relationship between goods and services, other recent work stresses the complementarity of growth in goods and services [Stanback, *et al.*, 1981; Shelp, 1981]. However, it emphasises the producer services as an input to goods production and will receive no further attention here. Gershuny treats producer services as an aspect of the increasing productivity of goods production.
4. In Gershuny's words [1983: 84], 'the contrast between the evolution of final demand for marketed services and the evolution of employment in marketed service industries is explained in part by the development of producer services [excluded here] and in part by the relatively low labour productivity growth rate in the service sector'.
5. Put more formally, a consumer will not devote any time to an activity if the substitution of time in a non-chosen activity for that spent in a chosen activity would make him/her worse off. At high levels of income, the budget constraint declines and the marginal utility of money for consumption may be zero; only the time constraint is effective. This theory departs from Lancaster [1966] in assuming that utility is not derived from properties of goods, but rather from the activities for which goods are used, similar to Gershuny's 'service function' concept.
6. Throwing away products one has no time to use or maintain is another solution to time constraints, but it is irrational continually to purchase goods which have no utility. Of course, if income is high enough, compulsive acquisition of goods may occur simply for the sake of ownership, but the utility is unrelated to consumption, and is rather a form of Hirschman's [1973] obituary-enhancement. Extra income may also be saved, rather than spent on goods. In this way, utility is spread more evenly over the life-cycle, postponing some consumption until periods when time is less expensive and scarce.
7. This is due to increased economies of scale, more intensive use of material means of consumption, and generally, below average wages of service workers.
8. Some final services have significant travel, management, search and set-up costs associated with them. Or they may not be available at precisely the hours the consumer wants them. This may prompt individuals to serve themselves for these particular functions rather than others. But service firms have started adjusting to these constraints, as in prolonged store and office hours or shopping by telephone or 24-hour a day automatic tellers. A micro-economic model asserts that when the sovereign consumer's demand is there, supply should meet it.
9. In recent years, the real level of women's wages has stagnated. However, so has that of men, making the opportunity costs of wives not working even greater with respect to maintaining family living standards. Possible supply-side reasons for increasing female labour force participation in the last decade include changing sex role socialisation, later age at marriage, lower fertility, higher divorce rates, and rising male unemployment. Indeed, in 1982, male unemployment exceeded female for the first time since 1950 [England, 1986: 150-2].
10. Comparability before 1940 is unreliable. In 1930, the Census had only 128 categories, most in manufacturing. In 1880 and 1900, only occupational statistics and not those on industry were collected. Despite a number of estimation techniques available to make categories from before this date comparable, they require a number of unrealistic assumptions or supplementary data sources [Miller and Brainerd, 1957; Lebergott, 1964; Carson, 1949]. Instead, this study reports industrial (sectoral) distributions by sex for 1910 and 1930 only, because these censuses did publish occupations within industries by sex, already allocating occupations in more than one industry. Although the

industrial classifications themselves differ, especially for the social and personal services, this method avoids many of the pitfalls of other methods.

11. This preponderance of women in part-time jobs appears to be much more marked in Britain than in other countries. O. Robinson and J. Wallace, 'Growth and Utilization of Part-Time Labour in Great Britain', *Employment Gazette* (September 1984).

12. As Oppenheimer [1970] notes, there was a substantial reduction of the burden of household work in the 1900–40 period as well as in the 1940–58 period – yet it is not until after 1940 that there was a radical change in the work rates of married women. If labour-saving devices were the most important factors in the situation, there should have been a gradual shift to this pattern as the mechanisation of the home advanced.

Moreover, cause-and-effect may be confused here. Contrary to Gershuny, who sees consumer goods as a motive for withdrawing from paid work, these goods have expanded the labour supply through the aspiration to obtain the income to purchase them. In fact, if there were no new 'needs' to expand consumption, leisure time should have expanded. In sum, women's labour force participation – primarily in the service sector – has made possible the expansion of the market for consumer goods, rather than the reverse.

13. A survey in 1981–82 indicated that husbands increased their contributions over the 1970s as well as between 1967 and 1976. In addition, there was a 22 per cent rise in the number of husbands keeping house between 1980 and 1982. Husbands also increase their housework slightly if they have an employed spouse [Berk and Berk, 1979; Bergmann, 1986].

14. In Britain, one-parent families are a smaller minority of all family households than in the US which may account for Gershuny's emphasis. However, such families have increased there as well, so that in 1984, one in eight families had only one parent [Haskey, 1986].

15. These categories are: 1. extractive (agriculture, forestry, fisheries and mining); 2. transformative (construction, manufacturing and utilities); 3. distributive services (transport, communications, wholesale and retail trade, excluding eating and drinking places); 4. producer services (finance, insurance, real estate, engineering, accounting, legal and business services); 5. social services (medical services, hospitals, education, welfare, non-profit agencies, postal and government services, and miscellaneous social services); 6. personal services (private households, hotels, eating and drinking places, repair services, laundries, barbers and beauty shops, entertainment and recreation, and miscellaneous personal services) [Singelmann, 1978]. The latter two categories are referred to here as 'consumer services'.

16. Similarly, in Britain, sport, catering and other consumer services have been among the fastest growing [Urry, 1987].

REFERENCES

Archambault, Edith, 1985 'Travail domestique et emploi tertiaire: substitution ou complémentarité?' in M. Vernières (ed.), *L'emploi du tertiaire*, Paris: *Economica*.

Becker, Gary, 1981, *A Treatise on the Family*, Cambridge, MA: Harvard University Press.

Becker, Gary, 1965, 'A Theory of the Allocation of Time', *Economic Journal*, Vol. 75, September.

Bergman, Barbara, 1986, *The Economic Emergence of Women*, New York: Basic.

Berk, Sarah F. and Richard Berk, 1979, *Labor and Leisure At Home: Content and Organization of the Household Day*, Beverly Hills: Sage.

Best, Fred, 1978, 'Exchanging Earnings for Leisure: Findings of an Exploratory National Survey on Work Time Preference', U.S. Department of Labor, Employment and Training Administration, R&D Monograph 79.

Brand, Horst and Ahmed Ziaul, 1986, 'Beauty and Barber Shops: The Trend of Labor Productivity', *Monthly Labor Review*, Vol. 109, March.

Carson, Daniel, 1949, 'Changes in the Industrial Composition of Manpower since the Civil

War', *Studies in Income and Wealth*, Vol. 11.

Deem, Rosemary, 1986, *All Work and No Play? The Sociology of Women's Leisure*, Milton Keynes: Open University Press.

Duclos, Denis, 1981, 'The Capitalist State and the Management of Time', pp. 164–82 in Michael Harloe and Elizabeth Lebas (eds.), *City, Class, and Capital: New Developments in the Political Economy of Cities and Regions*, London: Edward Arnold.

England, Paula, 1986, *Households, Employment and Gender*, New York: Aldine.

Evans, Alan W., 1972, 'On the Theory of the Valuation and Allocation of Time, *Scottish Journal of Political Economy*, Vol. 19, February.

Fisk, Donald M., 1985, 'Productivity Trends in the Federal Government', *Monthly Labor Review*, Vol. 108, October.

Faim, Paul O., 1986, 'Work Schedules of Americans: An Overview of New Findings', *Monthly Labor Review*, Vol. 109, Novermber: 3–6.

Gershuny, Jonathan, 1983, *Social Innovation and the Division of Labor*, New York: Oxford University Press.

Gershuny, Jonathan, 1978, *After Industrial Society: The Emerging Self-Service Economy*, London: Macmillan.

Gershuny, Jonathan and Ian Miles, 1983, *The New Service Economy: The Transformation of Employment in Industrial Societies* London: Frances Pinter.

Haskey, John, 1986, 'One-parent Families in Great Britain', *Population Trends*, 45, Autumn.

Herman, Arthur S., 1986, 'Productivity Continued to Increase in Many Industries During 1984', *Monthly Labor Review*, Vol. 109, March.

Hirschman, Albert O., 1973, 'Comment: Time in Economic Life', *Quarterly Journal of Economics*, Vol. 87, No. 4.

Katona, G., B. Strumpel, and E.Zahn, 1971, *Aspirations and Affluence*, New York: McGraw-Hill.

Lancaster, Kelvin, 1966, 'A New Approach of Consumer Theory', *Journal of Political Economy*, Vol. 74, March.

Lebergott, Stanley, 1964, *Manpower in Economic Growth: The American Record Since 1800*, New York: McGraw-Hill.

Linder, Steffan B., 1970. *The Harried Leisure Class*, New York: Columbia.

Miller, Ann Ratner and Carol P. Brainerd, 1957, 'Labor Force Estimates', *Population Redistribution and Economic Growth, United States, 1870–1950*. Vol I: Methodological Considerations and Reference Tables, Appendix A, Philadelphia, American Philosophical Society.

Oppenheimer, Valerie, 1970, *The Female Labor Force in the United States*, Westport, CT: Greenwood Press.

Parsons, Talcott, 1949, 'Social Structure of the Family', pp. 173–201 in Ruth Anshen (ed.), *The Family: Its Function and Destiny*, New York: Harper & Row.

Parsons, Talcott and R.F. Bales, 1955, *Family Socialization and Interaction Process*, New York: Free Press.

Personick, V.A., 1985, 'A Second Look at Industry Output and Employment Trends Through 1985', *Monthly Labor Review*, Vol. 108, November.

Presser, Harriet and Wendy Baldwin, 1980, 'Child Care as a Constraint on Employment: Prevalence, Correlates, and Bearing on the Work and Fertility Nexus', *American Journal of Sociology*, Vol. 85, No. 5.

Preteceille, Edmond and Jean-Pierre Terrail, 1985, *Capitalism, Consumption, and Needs*, London: Basil Blackwell.

Ruggie, Mary, 1984, *The State and Working Women: A Comparative Study of Britain and Sweden*, Princeton: Princeton University Press.

Schultz, T.W., 1981, *Investing in People*, Berkeley; University of California Press.

Schultz; T.W., 1974, *Marriage, Family, Human Capital, and Fertility, Journal of Political Economy*, Vol. 82, supplement.

Shank, Susan E., 1986, 'Preferred Hours of Work and Corresponding Earnings', *Monthly Labor Review*, Vol. 109, November.

Sharp, Clifford, 1981, *The Economics of Time*, Oxford: Martin Robertson.

Shelp, Ronald, 1981, *Beyond Industrialization: Ascendency of the Global Service Economy*,

New York: Praeger.

Silver, Hilary, Jean-Claude Delaunay and Jean Gadrey, 1986, 'La Question des Services aux Etats-Unis et en France', paper presented at the Colloque de Sociologie de Travail, CNRS, Paris, April.

Singlemann, Joachim, 1978, *From Agriculture to Services*, Beverley Hills: Sage.

Smith, Ralph E., 1979, 'Hours Rigidity: Effects on the Labor-Market Status of Women', pp. 211–22 in Karen Wolk Feinstein (ed.), *Working Women and their Families*, Beverly Hills: Sage.

Stanback, Thomas M., Peter J. Bearse, Thierry J. Noyelle and Robert A. Karasek, 1981, *Services: The New Economy*, Totowa, NJ: Allenheld, Osmun, & Co.

US Bureau of Labor Statistics, 1984, *Employment Projections for 1995*, Bulletin 2197, March.

US Bureau of the Census, 1986, *Statistical Abstract of the United States 1986*, Washington: GPO.

US Department of Labor, Women's Bureau, 1975, *1975 Handbook on Women Workers*, Bulletin 297.

Urry, John, 1987, 'Services: Some Issues for Analysis', *Society and Space*, Vol. 5.

Zaretsky, Eli, 1976, *Capitalism, The Family, and Personal Life*, New York: Harper & Row.

The Family and the Dynamics of Personal Services

by

Edith Archambault

The birthplace of personal services, often seen as activities where peripheral jobs can be created, is the family. Home production is more and more tertiary, and deserves a better knowledge, as the shift between domestic, marketed, collective and associative services is important and reversible. The demographic and sociological evolution of the family, the increase of female working activity, the greater plurality of family types implies more diversified and less standardised personal services. A kind of life cycle recourse to services can be observed and personal services of the future would be a patchwork of marketed, collective, associative and domestic services.

INTRODUCTION

In spite of the recent increase in the activity of both marketable and collective services, the family still remains without doubt the foremost enterprise when it comes to producing services in the industrialised countries, and even more so in developing countries. It is also the 'birthplace' of personalised services inasmuch as most of the services offered by the market economy, non-profit making institutions or public authorities have already been offered freely by the family. At a time when the creation of tertiary jobs is dwindling and can no longer offset the destruction of primary or secondary jobs, public authorities more or less throughout the industrialised countries are being induced to promote the creation of jobs of a derogatory status, peripheral and proximity jobs.

These 'small jobs', such as looking after young children, the aged or the handicapped, home deliveries and environment maintenance, are all service jobs and all come under marketed domestic work. Furthermore, they show some characteristics in common with domestic work: low qualification and rudimentary technology, lack of consideration and social marginalisation, flexibility and precariousness. The essential difference is obviously that peripheral jobs are paid, no matter how low the wage, whereas domestic work is not.

Inversely, the financial crisis of the welfare state leads to a situation in which those jobs that used to be carried out by the community are now returned to the family: domestic care of the sick, aged or handicapped can only be done with considerable domestic joint co-operation, whether it be done for free by a member of the sick person's family or by a home-help; the same is true of parental crèches. When young unemployed people carry on living at home, family services in kind replace or make up for insufficient unemployment benefits; the same acts of solidarity come into play between husband and wife. The tendency for the family to take minor risks is concurrent with the privatisation of collective insurance services.

First, we shall see that domestic production, which is essentially tertiary, is affected in unequal proportions by technical progress. Second, the onset of innovations affecting personal services could lead to modifications of job structure within market and collective services and a new distribution betwen socialised and non-socialised work. Third, we shall see what effects the present, foreseeable evolution of the family could have on the dynamics of services.

TERTIARISATION OF HOME PRODUCTION

Economic theories have, for a long time, shown no interest in the productive function of the family. It has always been studied as a consumption unit. Neo-classicists and Marxists agreed to see domestic production as an archaic carryover which would not resist market penetration and captialist production methods as far as consumer goods were concerned; thus domestic work appeared to be a labour reserve. As Marx put it:

> As some functions of the family, such as looking after and breast-feeding children cannot be totally suppressed, mothers are more or less forced to hire a replacement[1] since they feel held to ransom working in the system. Household jobs such as sewing, darning, etc. ... have to be replaced by ready-made goods. An increase in monetary expenditure corresponds to a decrease in domestic work [Marx, 1867: 941].

Considered from this angle, the production of goods by the family is thus transferred to industry, whereas the care of dependants – young children, the sick, handicapped and old people – is transferred to private individuals – 'replacements' and above all institutions.

This forecast has been partially borne out and partially contradicted. The increasing divergence in productivity between the agricultural and industrial sectors and domestic sector did indeed cause a transfer of the production of household goods towards the market economy which doubtless will be definitive: gardening for family produce has fallen off considerably and more among agricultural workers than other socio-professional groups, where it is more of a leisure activity. The manufacture of clothes, jams and food preserves at home has all but disappeared and that which still does subsist corresponds more to a need for expression or ecological considerations than economic preoccupations.

On the other hand, the transfer of service activities to the market and collective institutions has been much more partial and is not of an irreversible nature. Indeed, the key advantage of mass production which had been observed for goods exists for only a few services: those that demand highly qualified work, or that are likely to be rationalised and thus mass-produced, such as health services or teaching and insurance of financial services. On the contrary, for maintenance services or services for the repair of durable or semi-durable household goods and personal services, other than those previously cited, the relative advantage of the market or collective institutions has by no means been shown and self-production by the household remains, in all probabilities, considerable. This is most probably true, since it is still not known what is produced within households.[2] If the time spent on diverse domestic activities is known thanks to budget-time surveys (in France surveys into how people use their time were carried out by the INSEE in 1974 and 1985), what is not known is the precise nature and volume of production that result. Indeed, the productivity of domestic work, which varies according to the individuals, the equipment of the household, and the size of the family is not known. Nor are any references available concerning the time needed to accomplish everyday domestic chores. Paradoxically, the self-production of households which is taken into account in French national accounting, FF 282 billion in 1985 (that is 6.8 per cent of the GNP), represents for ten per cent the production of agricultural goods and foodstuffs consumed by agricultural-worker households. This has been declining sharply and the rest (90 per cent of the whole) is mostly composed of fictitious rents which householders, who own their accommodation, pay to themselves. So it is a service rendered by a durable good and does not correspond to any domestic activity. An essential part of the domestic production of developed countries, which is made up of maintenance and personal services, is therefore neglected by national accounting; the international convention on the measuring of self-production can, in effect, be explained by the relative importance of the self-consumption of foodstuffs in developing countries.

To bridge this gap, a statistical survey on domestic production is planned by the middle-term programme of the Conseil National de l'Information Statistique, and a seminary on this theme given by the National Centre of Scientific Research (CNRS) and the National Institute of Statistics and Economics (INSEE) in March 1986, brought to light the collective ignorance of the participants in this field. This research, the painstakingly slow progress of which bears witness to its lack of priority, should, in time, enable a better insight to be gained into the volume of goods and especially of services produced within households. These data concerning the output of domestic production will therefore be able to be combined with existing or future data on the time necessary to do domestic work, the use of durable household goods (at present only the numbers of those possessed is known) and the consumption of more or less sophisticated durable or semi-durable goods. In this way the functions of domestic production inspired by the theory of Becker and the new consumption theory of Lancaster could be reconstituted [Chadeau and Roy, 1986; Archambault, 1985].

These functions are by necessity complex, as they have a multiplicity of objectives: maximisation of use value, emotional and symbolic expression, affirmation of identity. They also have several constraints, of a budgetary and temporal nature, as the previously-quoted authors have noted, and also a spatial constraint. Domestic production indeed engenders an accumulation of activities at the same time.

As a preliminary, a nomenclature for domestic production must be proposed. The one which is proposed hereafter relies on the distinction between goods and services, as with nomenclature of activities and product (NAP): NAP is the French nomenclature but SIC (Standard Industrial Classification) would be relevant. Services are presented as in the NAP in increasing intangible order.

Domestic Production

1. *Production of goods*

    1.1. Gardening and domestic breeding (self-production).
    1.2. Other production of goods: clothes, food preserves, furniture, self-construction.

2. *Production of services relative to goods*

    2.1. Maintenance, repair and decoration of home
       211: Housework
       212: Handiwork
    2.2. Upkeep and repair of clothes and linen
       221: Washing
       222: Ironing
       223: Mending
    2.3. Upkeep of other durable goods (including car)
    2.4. Purchases (including transport, handling and storage).

3. *Production of services relative to persons*

    3.1. Preparation of meals
       311: Cooking and serving
       312: Table-laying
       313: Washing up
    3.2. Child care and education
       321: Washing and other material care
       322: Family education (including games, conversation, etc. . . .)
       323: Relations with the scholastic and parascholastic system (including transport).
    3.3. Care of other persons in the household (dependants or otherwise).
    3.4. Service rendered to persons outside the household (neighbourhood help or extended family).
    3.5. Services rendered to pets.

4. *Organisation and co-ordination of domestic work*

    4.1. Organisation of domestic work.

    4.2. Accounting and management of financial assets.

    4.3. Relations with public authorities (Inland Revenue, DHSS) and suppliers.

5. *Production of accommodation services* (fictitious rents)

Like that of Chadeau and Roy, this nomenclature adopts Hill's distinction between services which transform goods and services intended for persons [Hill, 1979]. Transport services are not isolated and are associated with the activities they concern. On the other hand, services which correspond to management activity are isolated. They are elementary when domestic work is limited to the reproduction of ancestral gestures. These organsation services assume an importance when the stock of durable goods of households increases, in the same way that their financial and real-estate patrimony is to manage, when relations with public authorities are increased and when child-education is personalised. Personal services are dispatched according to their addressee. Indeed, an indication of the extremely personalised and hierarchical character of these services can be seen on reading the names spontaneously noted by those questioned for the time-budget survey: there are several concentric family circles: in the epicentre are very young children and the sick, in a second circle the other members of the household, then the extended family, and finally the others.

TECHNOLOGICAL INNOVATIONS AND SHIFT OF ACTIVITIES

The domestic production vector tends to be displaced from activities situated at the beginning of the nomenclature towards those at the end. The technological innovations of the post-war years have contributed essentially to increasing productivity and decreasing the painstaking aspect of services relative to goods, as well as meal-preparing activities; some innovations, such as non-iron textiles or self-cleaning ovens, have even eliminated a few of these domestic activities.

    Recent innovations in the field of telecommunications (the generality of the telephone which makes up the infrastructure network, 89 per cent of French households being equipped with one in 1985, the spread of teletel and personal computers and the creation of local cable networks) allied to social innovations like the recent multiplication of very specialised users' associations, the spread of enterprises providing sophisticated material and technical advice, could, in the years to come, lead to a new distribution between domestic, marketed and collective services.

    Two examples are taken, that of teledistribution and that of keeping old people in the home. Whereas the modernisation and the concentration of the distribution sector has been accompanied by considerable development in self-service, that is to say a transfer of remunerated work consisting of customer advice, handling and delivery to domestic work (a transfer which is considered by Stoclet to be equivalent to the loss of 130,000 jobs [Stoclet,

1983], the recent developments in teletel long-distance ordering could result in the creation of skilled jobs in the telecomunications services and unskilled jobs in delivery, as well as modifications in the employment structures between salesmen and deliverymen. But for a telecommunications service to be adopted it is not enough for it to be proposed to a household with the necessary equipment at its disposal. The diffusion of this service will depend on the household's acceptance of the extra cost, that is to say the price implicit in the domestic work saved and also the necessity of choosing by referring to abstract characteristics without being able to appraise the quality by direct contact. It will also depend on the proportion of direct utility drawn from supply activity, that is to say from the leisure dimension which is more or less present in domestic work. A couple, for whom supermarket shopping constitutes an outing, will find it much more difficult to give it up than a single woman who sees it as a chore.

Keeping old and handicapped people at home, which is the alternative to putting them in hospital, presupposes the diffusion of more or less sophisticated equipment intended to assist in everyday life and electronic equipment for medical surveillance. It also requires a minimum of home-help and personal aid which can be given by the immediate family or, failing that, by salaried workers and by an associated network of specialists in material, medical and psychological support, capable of immediate intervention in case of distress. Here, too, there is a modification in the present structure of tertiary jobs: there is a transfer of hospital jobs towards skilled jobs in mobile medicine or in the maintenance of appliances, low-skilled jobs in home-help and personal care and benevolent work supplied, either by the family or by associations. Here, too, there is no technological determinism.

Resistance on the part of very structured professions which risk being affected by this evolution; resistance also on the part of families which can refuse to offer associated domestic work; difficulties in financial distribution between the interested party, the close family and the community, can all be opposed to an evolution which, no doubt, is desirable.

EVOLUTION OF THE FAMILY AND RECOURSE TO MARKETED AND COLLECTIVE SERVICES

Since the middle of the 1960s, the family in France, as in other industrialised countries, is undergoing a profound demographic change which should modify the demand of personal services and more generally, behaviour and life-styles.

The fall of the fertility rate below the generation replacement level, the prolonging of life and the decline in cohabitation of the different adult generations, together with the increase of divorce and one-parent families is causing a reduction in the size of households: 2.7 persons per household in 1982 in France, that is one person less than a century ago [Courson and De Saboulin, 1985]. The reduction in the size of households encourages recourse to outside services, for there are economies of scale in domestic production. On the other hand, it is to be observed that children, though fewer in numbers, stay at home longer, either to prolong their education or because they are unemployed. Leaving home by young people which continued up until 1975 was on the decline between 1975 and 1982. In the case of youth unemployment, local studies show that family solidarity works essentially in favour of the 15–19 age group much more than the 20–24 age group by permitting prolonged living at home or by other financial aid or help in kind [Barthe, 1985]. However significant this evolution may be, it cannot counterbalance the previous one which is much more considerable.

The drop in the number of marriages and the increase in unmarried couples and one-parent families all follow the tendency towards a greater recourse to outside services. Couples living together and one-parent families have, on average, a lesser patrimony at their disposal, are more often than not tenants and take more meals outside the home than married couples [Fouquet and Meron, 1982].

The increased incidence of single people living alone is an evolution correlated to the previous one: divorced persons remarry less and less, celibacy without cohabitation is increasing among men of underprivileged socio-professional groups (farm labourers and workers) and among women of high socio-professional groups (upper bracket executives and teachers). Lastly, and most significantly, the extension of life expectation and the excessive male mortality rate have multiplied the number of widowers and especially the number of widows living alone: 560,000 men over 60 and 2,100,000 women over 60 live alone [Audirac, 1985]. Whereas in 1962 aged persons living alone were less numerous than those living with close relatives, in 1982 they were twice as numerous. Only 4 per cent of the population over 60 live in an old people's home, hospice or retirement home, in spite of a very noticeable increase recently. By the year 2000, the INSEE forecasts that 7,000,000 French persons will be living alone. It will therefore be necessary to organise this solitude, as we have previously seen, and possible solutions include a complicated setting up of marketed, collective, associative and domestic services and a combination of public and private financing.

Thus a kind of life-cycle of recourse to services can be observed. Young people, single people or those living together are more often than not tenants, use public transport, frequently eat out and spend their leisure time going out. The constitution of the family is accompanied by a re-focusing on the domestic sphere with the acquisition of the principal durable goods and a domestic production as intense as the family is numerous. Those who fall into the category of old-age pensioners favour a return to marketed and collective services: public transport and in particular health services. Whatever their age, single men have greater recourse to marketed services and single women to domestic service [Glaude and Moutardier, 1982].

The considerable increase in the number of female salaried workers is without doubt the main factor influencing the recourse to outside services.

This process which has not been inflected by the crisis, contrary to what was previously observed, is not finished. If, at the present time in France, 71 per cent of women between the ages of 20 and 50 work, it is forecast that this pattern of female working activity will draw close to that of the male pattern, as can already be observed in Scandinavian countries. Projections for the year 2000 forecast female activity rates of 82.5 per cent. Even though it has recently been on the increase, the number of Frenchwomen who work part-time is relatively small: 20 per cent as against 30 per cent in West Germany, 50 per cent in the Netherlands, 41 per cent in the U.K., 44 per cent in Denmark [*Economie et Statistique*, 1986].

The expansion of female working activity can be observed for women of all generations and whatever the number of children. It poses the acute problem of looking after young children [Desplanques, 1985 and Leprince, 1986]: 900,000 children under three years of age have an active working mother. Community care of children is limited since there are only 80,000 places in the crèches: that is, one place for 30 children. At present it is the family which undertakes the bulk of the service, since two-thirds of children under three, that is to say 1,400,000, are cared for by their mother (who is either not working, independent or working at home), 120,000 are looked after at home by a member of the family and 150,000 outside the home. Care of other children is divided among the various kinds of childcare (domestic helpers, child nurses, etc.). Present and above all future needs in this field are therefore considerable and the problem to be resolved remains, as in the case of care of old or handicapped people, that of financing. The problems of looking after children over three years of age outside school time, during the holidays and minor illnesses has only been resolved to a very limited extent.

The result of the previous evolutions is the multiplicity of types of family which have specific needs in respect to personal services; these needs are met by different combinations of marketed, collective, associative or domestic services. The main types are the patriarchal family which is still relatively numerous, in which the woman remains at home and either helps an independent worker or does not work. This type of family is centred on cultivation of land, business or enterprise, possesses and transmits a relatively large patrimony and finds it easy to intermingle domestic production and enterprise production. These simultaneous activities are made easier by a unity of place. Similar to this type of family are the households of high socio-professional groups where the woman does not work. The type of family which is tending to become dominant is that of the stable working family, with no or few children, where both partners work. Among younger couples, simple household chores are shared and recourse to market or community services is great. The patrimony of these families consists essentially of housing. Also on the increase are single-parent families and those families in which remarriage or cohabitation has taken place, leading to more children, once the original couple has broken up.

The dynamics of personal services must therefore take into account the plurality of needs of a society which is more and more complex and less and less standardised.

NOTES

1. Thus the notion of 'third person' is to be found in Marx, which, in empirical studies on time-budget in households, enables a division to be made between productive activities (corresponding to domestic work) and unproductive activities (corresponding to leisure): a productive activity is one which can be put to work with a result comparable with an economic unit other than that which effectively realises it. Cf Hill [1979] and Chadeau and Roy [1986].

2. Chadeau and Fouquet [1971] measured domestic work according to three methods. The third and most ambitious method which they retained consists of obtaining the gross value of domestic production and, by the deduction of intermediary consumption and depreciation of the equipment, net added value which can be identified to the payment imputed to non-market work. In order to do this, the authors wanted to measure products made in the domestic sphere and estimate them to the value of market substitutes, by using essentially demographic indicators. In this way the number of meals served at home has been evaluated on the unit price of a meal served in a modest restaurant; the number of nights spent in residence, which are supposed to represent housework activities related to the lodgings, have been evaluated on the price of a hotel room of an equivalent nature. Unfortunately the method has its shortcomings, for in the case of other domestic activities, the goods produced are not known and the authors had to multiply the time spent on each activity by the corresponding wage rate for a skilled worker.

   Goldschmidt-Clermont [1983] uses the same kind of method for a fraction of domestic production identifiable by volume indicators: number of meals served, square metres cleaned, etc.

   These are the only 'direct' evaluations of domestic production available. All other measures rely on an evaluation of the time spent on domestic activities by a salary rate serving as a reference.

REFERENCES

Archambault, E., 1985, 'Travail domestique et emploi tertiaire, substitution ou complémentarité' in M. Vernières (ed.), *L'emploi du tertiaire*, Paris: *Economica.*

Audirac, P.A., 1985, 'Les personnes âgées: de la famille à l'isolement', *Economie et statistique*, no. 175.

Barthe, M.A., 1985, 'Pauvreté et politique sociale', Université de Paris I, Thèse, ronéotée.

Chadeau, A. and A. Fouquet, 1981, 'Peut-on mesurer le travail domestique?', *Economie et Statistique*, no. 137.

Chadeau, A. and C. Roy, 1986, 'Relating to Households final consumption to household activities: substitutability or complementarity between market and non-market production', *The Review of Income and Wealth*, series 32, no. 4.

Courson, J.P. and M. de Saboulin, 1985, 'Ménages et familles, vers de nouveaux modes de vie', *Economie et statistique*, no. 175.

Desplanques, G., 1985, 'Modes de garde et scolarisation des jeunes enfants', *Economie et statistique*, no. 176.

Economie et statistique, 1986, Special Issue, 'Les Français en l'an 2000', no. 190.

Fouquet, A. and M. Meron, 1982, 'Héritages et donations', *Economie et statistique*, no. 145.

Glaude, M. and M. Moutardier, 1982, 'L'évolution des niveaux de vie de 1966 à 1977', *Economie et statistique*, no. 142.

Goldschmidt-Clermont, L., 1983, 'Does Housework Pay? A product-related Microeconomic Approach', *Signs*, Chicago, autumn.

Hill, T.P., 1979, 'Do it yourself and GDP', *The Review of Income and Wealth*, series 25, no. 1.

Leprince, F., 1986, *L'accueil des jeunes enfants: les actions des comités d'entreprise et des associations parentales*, Paris: Laboratoire d'Economie Sociale, Université de Paris I.

Marx, K., 1867, *Le capital*, Paris: Editions Sociales.

Stoclet, D., 1983, 'Les transferts entre marchand et domestique. Travail des femmes, loisirs des hommes', *Observations et diagnostics économiques*, no. 3.

Time Use and the Dynamics of the Service Sector

by

Jonathan Gershuny

This article looks at the historical dynamics of service provision from a rather unusual perspective – the change in patterns of time use. It discusses a mechanism whereby activity patterns in 'the economy' may be accounted for in terms of time rather than money, and shows how this form of economic activity is associated with other ('extra-economic') sorts of productive and leisure activities. It presents time-budget data, from a number of different developed economies, showing historical changes in time allocation patterns, and relates these to more conventional indicators of economic structure.

THE MARCH THROUGH THE SECTORS

The familiar, post-Second World War model of economic development gave a rather special status to the service sector. Services were the goal, the *end*, of development. Material needs being satisfied, work would increasingly consist of the clean and civilised business of providing services for our fellow citizens. We had once been workers of the soil, we have passed through a phase where most of us worked in factories, and, as we escape (through technical improvements in the efficiency of production) from the 'realm of necessity', we arrive at the service millennium. Here, economic life is not dominated by the production and consumption of material objects, but by the mutual exchange of intangibles – work, in this Elysian version of the Service Economy, consists of activities which directly change other peoples' personal circumstances, mental or physical states or conditions. Productivity growth, first in the primary, then in the secondary sectors of the economy, combined with a proportional shift of final demand away from basic material necessities and towards the more luxurious intangibles, hastens the emergence of the post-industrial, post-materialist era of plenty. The post-industrial syllogism runs thus: wealth means service consumption, and service consumption requires service production, *therefore*, wealthy societies are dominated by service employment.

For a number of years I have been engaged in the construction of an alternative account of the dynamics of the succession of the sectors or branches of developed economies. I have argued that two particular sorts of techno-organisational change serve to disturb this smooth transition to a post-industrial millennium. One is innovation in the mode of acquisition of final services: rather than buying some sorts of services, consumers buy equipment and materials, which they use to produce final services within their own households – 'self-servicing' replacing the consumption of purchased services. The other is a sort of reversal of the process of vertical integration in industrial production; the development and growth in importance of specialised intermediate services, services provided not to consumers but to other producers. In this alternative account, the growth of service employment is in large part explained by innovations in the processes of the production of material goods (i.e., increase in the 'producer services' rather than 'consumer services'). And the purchasing of final material goods by consumers tends, if anything, to increase as a proportion of national income. Service workers contribute to the efficient production of goods; consumers buy the goods, and use them to produce services for themselves.

The evidence used previously to demonstrate the argument was ali drawn from conventional economic statistics. I have shown, for example, how the balance of household expenditure on entertainment has shifted proportionately away from purchased entertainment services (e.g., going to the cinema or theatre) towards expenditure on entertainment goods (e.g., compact disc players, TVs, videos) – from which we may infer that an increasing proportion of all final entertainment services are produced within the household economy rather than in the formal economy. I have also shown that real value added by service industries has grown very much faster than real final consumption (including direct government provision) of services – the implication must be that a large part of the growth of value added is intermediate to the production of goods.

Two conclusions emerge from this line of argument. The first concerns the ambiguity in the conceptualisation of 'services'. Services as an industrial sector obviously covers something other than 'services' as a category of final consumption; we need to relate activity in 'the economy' more closely to the sorts of human purposes to which they contribute. Rich economies *are* dominated by service employment and value added but not in the uncomplicated way suggested by the post-industrial syllogism. We must develop a system of accounts that adequately represents the complexities of the relationship between the 'service sector' and the final consumption of services. The second conclusion is that, if we are to understand the processes of structural change in 'the economy', we need to consider evidence about behaviour outside it: we need to know more about the detail of daily life. To understand the operations and historical dynamics of the development of service provision, we need evidence of what people do with the goods and services that they buy.

Economic statistics, unsurprisingly, describe just 'the economy'. But there is a technique for collecting quantitative statistical evidence about the household economy: the *time budget survey*. This article outlines one way that time budget data can be used to extend our understanding of the dynamics of service provision. It suggests a new way of organising socio-economic accounts, using time rather than money as a *numeraire*. And it very briefly summarises the intermediate results of a study which yields some clues about how current new technologies may be expected to affect the structure of employment over the coming decades.

TIME-USE AND CHAINS OF PROVISION

The conventional time budget shows the individual's allocation of his or her own time to a range of activities – perhaps some paid work, some unpaid work in the home, some leisure activities, some sleep and personal care. This is the individual's own time; but of course the individual additionally uses other people's time. All the goods and services used by one individual derive from the work time of others. So an alternative way of organising time use accounts is to consider, not how individuals spend *their own* time, but how individuals use time – their own or other people's – for their own purposes.

Consider, for example, food. We spend some of our time in consuming it, some more of our time preparing it for eating (cooking) – and we spend money to buy the raw materials and equipment and utensils we use in the course of preparing and eating it. Embodied in the materials and commodities we buy is the paid work time of other people (and perhaps a very small part of our own paid work time). The individual's level of nutrition results from the combination of his or her own consumption and unpaid work time (eating and cooking) with the paid work time of farmers and fishermen and manufacturing and transport and retail and other service workers.

We might consider three distinct broad categories of time: paid work time, unpaid work time and leisure/consumption time. Each individual's state of material well-being results from the combination of these. There is a 'chain' of provision – or perhaps a better metaphor might be a complex interwoven net of threads of provision – passing from the farmer (and before the farmer, from the workers in agrochemical industry, farm vehicle manufacturing and so on) through manufacturing process workers who prepare and package the food, lorry drivers who transport it, workers in retail industry who sell to households, and then the unpaid work in households, preparing the food to be eaten, and finally the consumption of the food. Each link in the chain can be accounted for in terms of one of the three sorts of time use. Add together each link in the chain and we have the total time the society devotes to nutrition. And similarly we can think of other purposes – shelter, entertainment, education and so on – each of which has its own chain of provision, its own thread of paid work, unpaid work and consumption. Every activity in the society may be defined as having a place in one such chain of provision.

This way of looking at the world demands a new form of accounts, organised around a classification of human purposes. By 'purposes' I do not mean any ultimate or transcendent goals or needs such as love or security or power, but rather, the much shorter-term day by day purposes of economic activity, such as the acquisition of food or entertainment or medical services. Any classification of purposes will inevitably give rise to arguments about means and ends. (Are not 'housing' and 'clothing' both means to the same ends?) In this case, however, such arguments are not really to the point: the classification is no more than a means for linking together the chain of provision, for associating particular sorts of paid work with particular sorts of unpaid work and consumption. The paid work time of the farmers *is* clearly linked with the time spent cooking and washing up, and the time spent in eating; we need a system of accounts which registers these connections.

A SYSTEM OF ACCOUNTS

The notion of 'chains of provision' provides a straightforward basis for such a system of socio-economic accounts which includes consumption time and unpaid work as well as employment. We can relate time-use outside paid employment, to final expenditure on (or state provision of) goods and services, and hence to employment. And since both paid employment and extra-economic activities may be measured in terms of time, we arrive at a time-based account of changes in lifestyle and economic structure.

The first step relies on the observation that each sort of activity is associated with the use of particular final goods and services. Time spent at the cinema requires the purchase of entry, travel time requires a passenger ticket, time at school requires either state expenditure on a final service, or more occasionally, some household expenditure on private education. Washing clothes may require laundry services, or household expenditure on soap, water rates, electricity, a washing machine, and a service contract for it. Each time-use category is associated with a distinct bundle of goods and services (though of course each category of goods or service may be associated with more than one category of activity – the same kitchen table may be used for food preparation, and for eating and for school homework).

In principle, these associations between activity categories and the commodities used while engaged in them, could be determined empirically. We could, for example, ask within the time budget diary, not only 'What were you doing? Where? With whom?' but also 'Using what?'. In practice, of course, such a research instrument would be quite unmanageable but the same end could be achieved by other, observational techniques. For the moment, however, as a first pass through the sequence of analysis, I have allocated commodities to their appropriate activities purely on the basis of *a priori* reasoning; Table 1 summarises this set of assumptions.

These associations between activities and commodities are crucial in forming the link between the time-budget 'lifestyle' indicators, and conventional economic statistics. The time expenditure categories in Table 1 include the full range of activities other than paid work; the money expenditure categories cover all the sorts of final goods and services

TABLE 1

ACTIVITIES, TIME USE AND RELATED EXPENDITURES

Time-Use Activities (mean min.per ave. day) ("forty categories")	Goods (Family Expenditure Survey)	Marketed Services (Family Expenditure Survey)	Non-market Services (National accounts)
Shelter/Clothing	Housework	Housing (rent,rates,other charges), power and fuel, clothing, furniture (inc. cutlery, china, and oddments) cleaning materials, matches, etc.	Repairs,maintenance,decoration, household etc insurance, laundry and cleaning, domestic help, other repairs not allocated elsewhere	Sewerage, Refuse disposal, Fire, Local welfare, and other welfare services
Food: Cooking	Cooking, washing-up			Agriculture, fishing & food
Meals	Eating meals, snacks	All food and non-alcoholic drinks.		
Childcare	Child care			Childcare
Shopping	Shopping			
Travel : Domestic & Comms: Other	Domestic travel Leisure travel and excursions	Postage,telephones,telegrams; purchase of car, bicycle, etc.	Maintenance and running costs of motor vehicles, bus,train fares,etc	Roads, Lighting, Transport & Communications
Personal Care	Dressing, toilet, sleep.	Toilet requisites, cosmetics	Hairdressing	
Restuarants	Restuarants		Meals bought away from home	
Pubs	Pubs and social clubs	Alcoholic drink		
Cinema,Theatre	Cinema, theatre, dances, parties, etc; at church; civic duties; watching sports.		Cinemas, theatres and other events	Libraries, museums, etc.
Playing Sports	Playing sports			
Walking	Walks			
Visiting/Entertaining	Entertaining or visiting friends			
TV, Radio	TV, radio, music	Radio and television, and musical instruments (including repairs)	Radio and television licences and rental payments	
Reading,Study	Reading books or papers, or studying	Books, magazines and periodicals		
Talking,Relaxing	Conversation, relaxing	Cigarettes, tobacco, pipes etc.		
Oddjobs,Gardening	Oddjobs, gardening	Seeds, plants, flowers, and pets		
Games,Hobbies	Hobbies and pastimes, knitting, sewing			
Holidays			Hotel and holiday expenses, and miscellaneous other services	
Medical Services	Personal services	Medicines and surgical goods	Medical, dental, and nursing fees	N.H.S.
Education			Educational and training expenses	Education
Admin./Defence			Pocket money and other expenditure assigned elsewhere; life assurance pension contributions; sickness and accident insurance, savings of all kinds, including contributions to Christmas and holiday clubs	Defence, External Relations, Employment services, Research and Other Industry, Police & Prisons, Parliament, Finance, Records, and Other Services

consumed in the economy. The Table thus enables us to 'translate' time-use into final demand – and using the conventional economic statistical sources (input/output and industry/occupation matrices), we can in turn 'translate' final demand into industrial output, industrial employment, and thence into occupational employment patterns. (This process of 'translation' is a non-trivial task, requiring an intricate sequence of calculations which I shall not attempt to outline here; the general principle is nevertheless quite straightforward, and the set of associations in Table 1 is really the only unconventional aspect of it.)

Employment is itself a time-use category; furthermore, it is the one category missing from Table 1. So, in the time-use column of Table 1 we have all the activities other than paid work; and the money expenditure columns may be 'translated' into time spent at work in different occupations. We can, in short, replace Table 1 by an alternative formulation, which represents all the society's activities, inside and outside 'the economy', in terms of a single indicator, time.

Table 2 provides a very simplified version of such a system of accounts, which divides paid work summarily into just two categories, manual and non-manual. For each of the two years, the time-use columns add up to a total of 1440 minutes of the 'average' day of the population (aged 14+). In 1961, for example, this average day was made up of 236 minutes paid work, 989 minutes of leisure or consumption time (if we were to look at more detailed activity data, we would find that it includes 560 minutes of sleep and 98 minutes of eating) and 215 minutes of instrumental activity (cooking, cleaning, shopping, etc.) – which I summarily classify as unpaid work. The Table is organised around six groups of activities or 'purposes', of which two ('shelter, household maintenance', 'shopping, travel') involve just instrumental activities, two involve only consumption activities ('out-of-home leisure', 'medicine and education') and two ('home leisure, childcare', and 'food, sleep') include a mixture of unpaid work and non-work activities. Most of the paid employment in the economy can be 'explained' in terms of the final demand for commodities associated with these six classes of activities.

Most, but not all: we have to take into account, in addition, employment associated with foreign demand for UK products – which generates in all 38 minutes of the total of 236 minutes of paid work in the average UK day, but is not related to any unpaid work or consumption time in the UK. (Of course, these exports are related to consumption time in foreign countries – and similarly, some UK consumption time is related to expenditure on imports, which serve to 'explain' some foreign employment. The column headed 'foreign work' estimates this effect; the 40 minutes of 'foreign work' related to UK activities – which I have estimated crudely by assuming that the productivity levels in countries exporting to the UK are on average the same as those in the UK – approximately balance the 38 minutes of UK work associated with foreign consumption activities.)

Another category of UK production which cannot be matched with particular consumption or domestic work activities, is the provision of 'background' or 'environmental' services: law and order, defence, public administration, the effects of which are diffused through all of our experiences. (An alternative way of handling these might be to treat them as an 'intermediate product' with costs distributed evenly across all branches of production.) For the purposes of Table 2 I have grouped these in a single category together with employment associated with the provision of analogous private 'background' services such as life insurance, pensions and personal savings.

Consider the change, over the period 1961–84, in the 'shelter maintenance' chain. Unpaid work in this category, for the adult population as a whole, has fallen by about 15 minutes per average day. This is the phenomenon I have previously described as 'social innovation' in the provision of domestic services. I have argued that the largest part of this

TABLE 2

A TIME-BASED SYSTEM OF ACCOUNTS

mins per average day

	Time outside Employment		Time in Employment		All Paid Work In U.K.	Foreign Work from Imports	All Employmt '000s	Distrib. of Employmt
	Nonwork	Work	White Collar Work	Manual Work				
1961								
Shelter, Household	0	93	25	36	61	14	6278	.26
Food, Sleep etc	659	68	16	24	40	10	4123	.17
Home leisure, Chil	268	12	7	10	16	4	1672	.07
Shopping, Travel	0	41	6	7	13	1	1344	.06
Out-of-home Leisure	45	0	8	3	11	2	1169	.05
Medicine, Education	16	0	20	7	27	2	2814	.12
Background Service	0	0	15	14	29	1	3018	.12
Exports	0	0	13	25	38	6	3919	.16
All Time-Use	989	215	110	126	236	40	24337	1.00
1983								
Shelter, Household	0	73	25	21	46	16	5591	.24
Food, Sleep etc	647	63	8	8	16	6	1934	.08
Home leisure, Chil	284	17	7	5	12	3	1411	.06
Shopping, Travel	0	70	5	4	9	2	1119	.05
Out-of-home Leisure	70	0	9	2	11	2	1386	.06
Medicine, Education	22	0	30	5	36	3	4347	.18
Background Service	0	0	17	7	24	1	2951	.13
Exports	0	0	19	21	39	10	4824	.20
All Time-Use	1023	224	120	73	193	43	23564	1.00
Change 1961-1983/4								
Shelter, Household	0	-21	0	-15	-15	2	-687	-.02
Food, Sleep etc	-12	-5	-7	-17	-24	-4	-2189	-.09
Home leisure, Chil	15	5	0	-5	-5	0	-261	-.01
Shopping, Travel	0	29	-1	-3	-4	0	-225	-.01
Out-of-home Leisure	24	0	1	-1	0	0	217	.01
Medicine, Education	6	0	10	-2	8	1	1533	.07
Background Service	0	0	2	-7	-5	0	-66	.00
Exports	0	0	6	-5	1	4	905	.04
All Time-Use	34	9	10	-53	-43	3	-773	.00

reduction can be explained in terms, not of demographic structure or the role of women in the waged labour market, but by the increased use of 'labour-saving' equipment in households. (And in fact there is evidence for a very similar trend in domestic work time in the USA, Canada, Holland, Denmark and Norway; see Figure 1.) The reduction in unpaid work was enabled by increases in households' purchases of capital equipment and materials. The reduced housework time is in effect 'purchased' by an increase in domestic equipment. Though less time was spent in the unpaid 'instrumental' non-market tasks (indeed precisely *because* less time was spent in them) unpaid work time became more intensive in its demand for purchased commodities, and hence paid work.

So in spite of very high rates of productivity growth (an approximately three-fold increase) in the manufacturing sector over the period, paid work time related to this category of 'purpose' did not fall very fast (compared, for example, with paid work related to food, where increase in agricultural and manufacturing productivity was not balanced by increasing consumption intensity). Indeed, when we consider that the normal hours of work per employee actually fell by about 10 per cent over the period, we find that the number of jobs only declined by about 0.5 million from the 1961 total of 6.1 million, and white-collar and other service work associated with the provision of shelter has risen over the period we are considering. Thus, associated with this purpose, and as a result of the process of social innovation I have described, less time spent in unpaid production, but providing overall very nearly as many paid jobs in 1984 as in 1961.

Of course, the time freed from unpaid domestic work, and from the reduction in employed people's paid work time, must be spent somehow. One use to which this extra time is put is in the consumption of out-of-home recreational, educational, medical services. This sort of change does not involve increasing consumption intensity (i.e. increased expenditure and hence paid employment per moment of consumption time), but rather the increase of the total of time devoted to activities in which consumption intensity remains constant. A 'sit-down' meal at a restaurant, for example, involves just about as much labour time now as it did 30 years ago; but more people eat out in the 1980s than in 1961, which means more consumption time and hence more paid labour time. (Though the argument is complicated by the emergence of the 'fast food' industry over this period.) In the chain of provision of 'shelter', a reduction of the total of unpaid work time was balanced by an increase in the consumption intensity of that time, so that levels of paid employment hardly fell in spite of very substantial increases in labour productivity; in the 'out of home leisure' category – pubs, restaurants, sports – an increase in time devoted to *'time extensive'* service consumption leads to an increase in jobs. And a similar process may serve to explain the growth in employment in the chain of provision connected with medical and educational services.

Consider, finally, the 'shopping and related travel' category. Time spent by consumers in this activity has increased from about 45 minutes per average adult in 1961, to about 70 minutes in 1984. And as we see from Figure 2, this corresponds to similar increase in a number of other European countries. The North American data in Figure 2 are at a higher overall level, but do not show the same upward trend; the explanation of the increase seems to be innovation in the retail industry, leading to larger, self-service shops, in which the shopper spends more time selecting and paying for goods, shops which are geographically removed from town centres, which means more travel time (some alternative explanations are

FIGURE 1

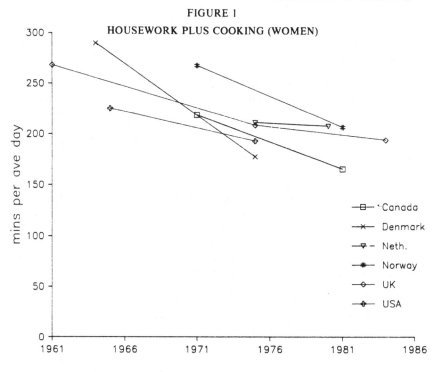

HOUSEWORK PLUS COOKING (WOMEN)

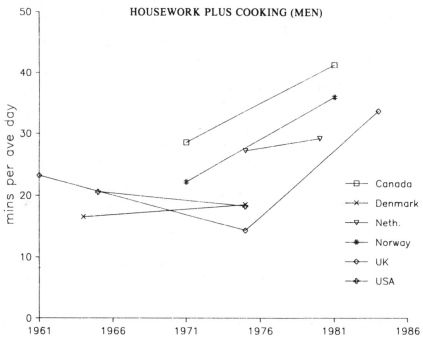

HOUSEWORK PLUS COOKING (MEN)

FIGURE 2

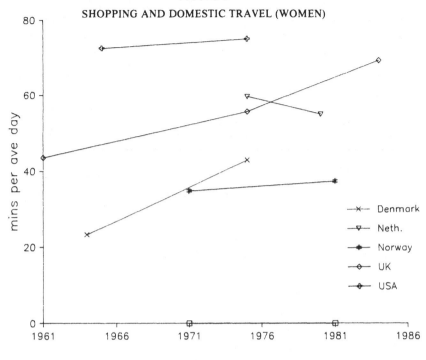

SHOPPING AND DOMESTIC TRAVEL (WOMEN)

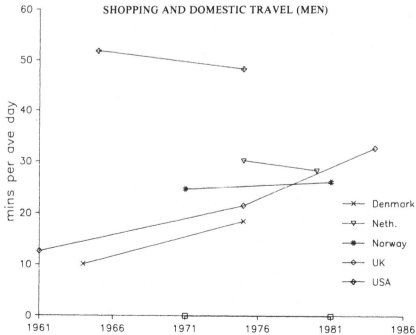

SHOPPING AND DOMESTIC TRAVEL (MEN)

discussed in Gershuny 1986). The lower prices of goods bought from super- or hyper-markets are in effect paid for by the increased non-money 'transaction costs' the increased time spent in shopping. We might, from a European prospective, interpret the multinational comparative evidence in Figure 2 as the Americanisation of retail distribution.

The very substantial amounts of time devoted to shopping and related activities, suggests a likely future effect of technical innovation on time use. The new technologies of the 1930s, valves, small electric motors, plastics, were embodied in consumer durable goods (washing machines, vacuum cleaners and the like) used in innovative 'informal' modes of provision of domestic services, which led to new jobs, and a reduction of unpaid work time from the 1940s to the 1970s. Might not the new technologies of the 1980s, microchips, fibre optics, be embodied in new ways of organising the provision of retail services? Tele-shopping, ordering goods from computer terminals in homes, making use of a range of associated services (consumer advice, funds transfers, home delivery, for example) could substantially reduce the amount of time currently devoted to marketing, and increase paid employment associated with the 'distribution' chain. And just as, in the past, time freed from domestic work went in part to enable the consumption of time extensive leisure services, so in the future might time freed from the burden of shopping.

CHAINS OF PROVISION V SECTORS OF THE ECONOMY

The Standard Industrial Classification (SIC) provides a structure for our mental images of our economies. Yet what has been said so far suggests that, it is not the most helpful of constructs. We know that the 'service sector' has been growing, in every country; but the conventional classification does not tell us how this growth relates to final production and consumption. We cannot understand the evolution of this 'branch' of the economy, other than in the context of its relationship to other 'branches', and the use made of the products of the economy in daily life.

The notion of 'chains of provision' by contrast, allows us to relate the different sorts of work done in the economy, to the pattern of life outside the economy. And this classification in turn allows us to explain the dynamics of structural change in a quite straightforward manner. We can in fact arrive at a reasonably good account of socio-economic structural change, in terms of *three processes*.

Table 3 is a slightly more disaggregated version of the UK evidence in Table 2. 'Managers, scientists, etc.', together with 'other producer services' (i.e., clerical and distributive trades) are all 'service' or 'white-collar' jobs. But they do not provide final services to consumers, and they might be jointly categorised as 'intermediate service workers'; they contribute service elements to a production sequence that might result in the supply of either a good or a service to final consumers. By contrast, the 'consumer service professions' (i.e. medics, teachers, artists, musicians) and the 'other consumer services' (catering, cleaning, security) do produce final services

TABLE 3 (Part 1)

OCCUPATIONAL STRUCTURE AND CHAINS OF PROVISION, UK 1961–1983/4

mins per average day

	Time outside Employment		Time in Employment						All Time Use
	Nonwork	Work	Managers Scientist etc	Other Producer Services	Consumer Service Professio	Other Consumer Services	Other Workers	All Paid Work	
1961									
Shelter, Household Ops	0	93	8	13	1	4	36	61	154
Food, Sleep etc	659	68	5	9	0	1	24	40	768
Home leisure, Childcare	268	12	2	3	0	1	10	16	296
Shopping, Travel	0	41	1	2	1	2	7	13	54
Out-of-home Leisure	45	0	1	1	0	6	3	11	57
Medicine, Education	16	0	2	3	10	5	7	27	44
Background Services	0	0	4	7	1	4	14	29	29
Exports	0	0	4	7	0	2	25	38	38
All Time-Use	989	215	27	45	14	24	126	236	1440
1983									
Shelter, Household Ops	0	73	8	12	2	3	21	46	119
Food, Sleep etc	647	63	3	4	0	1	8	16	727
Home leisure, Childcare	284	17	2	3	1	1	5	12	313
Shopping, Travel	0	70	1	2	0	1	4	9	79
Out-of-home Leisure	70	0	1	2	0	6	2	11	81
Medicine, Education	22	0	3	5	15	8	5	36	58
Background Services	0	0	5	7	1	4	7	24	24
Exports	0	0	7	9	1	3	21	39	39
All Time-Use	1023	224	30	43	20	27	73	193	1440
Change 1961–1983/4									
Shelter, Household Ops	0	-21	1	-1	0	0	-15	-15	-36
Food, Sleep etc	-12	-5	-2	-4	0	-1	-17	-24	-41
Home leisure, Childcare	15	5	0	-1	0	0	-5	-5	16
Shopping, Travel	0	29	0	0	0	-1	-3	-4	25
Out-of-home Leisure	24	0	0	0	0	1	-1	0	24
Medicine, Education	6	0	2	2	4	2	-2	8	14
Background Services	0	0	1	0	0	1	-7	-5	-5
Exports	0	0	3	2	0	1	-5	1	1
All Time-Use	34	9	4	-2	6	3	-53	-43	0

directly for the consumer. And the 'other workers' category covers all skilled and unskilled manual occupations not included elsewhere. We can illustrate the three processes from the data in Table 3.

The first process is of *change in the quantity and occupational distribution of paid labour associated with each chain of provision*. We see, in the second part of the table, a quite regular pattern of change in the division of paid work between the occupations across the various chains of provision. In every case, the manual component in the chain is substantially

TABLE 3 (Part 2)

CHANGE IN CHAINS OF PROVISION, 1961-1983/4

	Proportion of all Free Time		Prop. of Paid Work Time in each Chain					Prop. of All Paid Work	Prop. of All Time Use
	Nonwork	Unpaid Work	Managers Scientist etc	Other Producer Services	Consumer Service Professio	Other Consumer Services	Other Workers		
1961									
Shelter, Household Ops	.00	.08	.12	.21	.02	.06	.58	.26	.11
Food, Sleep etc	.55	.06	.13	.22	.01	.03	.61	.17	.53
Home leisure, Childcare	.22	.01	.12	.21	.02	.06	.59	.07	.21
Shopping, Travel	.00	.03	.10	.18	.04	.12	.55	.06	.04
Out-of-home Leisure	.04	.00	.07	.13	.02	.49	.28	.05	.04
Medicine, Education	.01	.00	.06	.12	.37	.19	.26	.12	.03
Background Services	.00	.00	.14	.23	.03	.13	.47	.12	.02
Exports	.00	.00	.10	.17	.01	.04	.67	.16	.03
All	.82	.18	.11	.19	.06	.10	.54	1.00	1.00
1983									
Shelter, Household Ops	.00	.06	.18	.26	.04	.07	.46	.24	.08
Food, Sleep etc	.52	.05	.18	.27	.02	.04	.48	.08	.50
Home leisure, Childcare	.23	.01	.17	.24	.06	.10	.42	.06	.22
Shopping, Travel	.00	.06	.16	.23	.05	.10	.47	.05	.06
Out-of-home Leisure	.06	.00	.09	.14	.03	.57	.18	.06	.06
Medicine, Education	.02	.00	.10	.13	.41	.21	.15	.18	.04
Background Services	.00	.00	.20	.29	.05	.18	.29	.13	.02
Exports	.00	.00	.17	.22	.01	.07	.53	.20	.03
								.00	
All	.82	.18	.16	.22	.10	.14	.38	1.00	1.00
Change 1961-1983/4									
Shelter, Household Ops	.00	-.02	.05	.05	.02	.01	-.13	-.02	-.02
Food, Sleep etc	-.03	-.01	.05	.06	.01	.01	-.13	-.09	-.03
Home leisure, Childcare	.00	.00	.05	.03	.04	.05	-.16	-.01	.01
Shopping, Travel	.00	.02	.06	.04	.01	-.03	-.08	-.01	.02
Out-of-home Leisure	.02	.00	.02	.01	.01	.07	-.10	.01	.02
Medicine, Education	.00	.00	.03	.02	.04	.02	-.11	.07	.01
Background Services	.00	.00	.05	.06	.02	.05	-.18	.00	.00
Exports	.00	.00	.06	.05	.01	.02	-.14	.04	.00
All	.00	.00	.04	.03	.04	.04	-.16	.00	.00
All Time-Use									
1961	.69	.15	.02	.03	.01	.02	.09	.16	1.00
1983/4	.71	.16	.02	.03	.01	.02	.05	.13	1.00
Change	.02	.01	.00	.00	.00	.00	-.04	-.03	.00

reduced. In five of the eight cases (shelter, foods, shopping and associated travel, exports, and background infrastructural services), the lost manual work is largely substituted by *producer services* – a growth in the intermediate, technical and information elements of the production process. In the remaining three cases (leisure, medical and educational provisions) as we might expect, the largest proportional increase is in the final service occupations. Associated with the change in occupational structure is a decrease in the labour required per unit of output: this process reflects the increase in the quantity of capital and in the efficiency of systems of production. (Obviously, at this level of aggregation, part of the change in the occupational structure also reflects changes in the balance of activities within each chain: thus, for example, the increase in the 'other consumer services' in the 'out-of-home leisure' chain, reflects the increasing part played by 'eating out' in restaurants in UK leisure patterns over this period.)

We should note that this process compounds two closely connected classes of change which are kept artificially distinct in the conventional sectoral classification. On one hand there is the change in occupational structure within particular industries. On the other, is the pattern of vertical integration, intermediate production and subcontracting in a particular chain of provision. The 'production genealogy' of any commodity will involve a series of component steps or stages. These various steps may all be completed within one firm and hence (by the accounting conventions of the ISIC) within one industry and one 'branch of the economy'. Or they may involve many firms, and hence perhaps various different branches. Which of these cases apply depends on particularities of national law, geography, history, and conditions of international trade. The same 'production genealogy' might be represented differently across various countries, or over time, as a result of cross-national or intertemporal variations in these circumstances. It is only by combining data on the occupational structure *within* industries with evidence on the 'input-output' relationships *between* industries that we arrive at a reliable basis for comparing the real, material processes of production involved in each chain of provision.

Note the final lines of the second part of the table, which shows the overall distribution of time between the various activities. Despite a very substantial reduction in the overall total of adult paid work in the UK (amounting to an 18 per cent decline in the total of paid work time since 1961) the absolute amount of time spent in service-type tasks remains unchanged, at about 8 per cent of the average adult day; time spent in the 'other manual' category by contrast has been virtually halved, from about 9 per cent of the average day, to 5 per cent. Note also that the 'intermediate service' activities continue to outweigh 'final services', by a proportion of about five to three.

The second process is of *change in the mode of provision for particular purposes*. This is the 'social innovation' mentioned previously: new products (or changed relative prices) encourage a change in the technical means and organisation that households or individuals employ to satisfy their wants or requirements. So, in the past, new household capital equipment reduced the demand for purchased final domestic services. So in the future, new technologies may be expected to enable or encourage changes in the distribution of occupations involved in the supply of retail services. The effect of this process is not, however, simply a matter of changing the quantity and mix of paid work associated with particular chains; there are also effects on the nature and quantity of unpaid work. While 'social innovation' may on occasion be driven in part by considerations of money cost (e.g. falling costs of household equipment vs increasing costs of domestic labour), it may also be driven additionally or alternatively by the desire to save time. In mass-consumption societies (which must, for economic stability, require continuous growth of consumption at a rate equivalent to the rate of growth of productivity) time (for consumption) will be at an increasing premium. Social innovations which achieve a reduction of unpaid work time through an increase in expenditure on goods (and hence an increased employment in their production) are obviously most desirable.

The third process is of *shifts in the overall distribution of time between purposes*. Time freed from paid and unpaid work by the foregoing processes, must be spent somehow: we see from the second part of Table 3 that over the 24-year period, about 5 per cent of all adult time was shifted out of the basic food and shelter categories, into the more sophisticated consumption of services. The first two processes tend, if anything, to reduce time spent providing for the 'basic' human purposes; technical and organisational innovations make the chains of provision more efficient. The chains associated with out-of-leisure and education have not (yet) been substantially affected by innovation; so we see in Table 3 that increases in consumption time devoted to these activities also have the consequence of increasing the associated paid work time. (I should add that the terms 'basic' and 'luxury' or 'sophisticated' do not represent any strong presumption of a hierarchy of human needs, but only a consequence of my particular classificatory schema; so, for example, a large part of the increase in out-of-home leisure time in the UK is explained by the increase in restaurant meals and social activities in pubs which might alternatively have been allocated to the 'food' category.)

CONCLUSION

Ultimately, what determines economic structure is society's style of life. The model outlined in this article shows how lifestyle (in the quite concrete sense of the allocation of time between alternative activities) can be related systematically to demand for products from the formal economy, and hence to paid employment, and how technical innovations affect the relationship between activity patterns and final demand. The conventional three-sector model of the evolution of economic structure, based on the work of Fisher, Clark and Fourastie, dating back nearly 50 years, is not really very helpful for understanding the sorts of structural changes which now face us. An approach based on the notion of 'chains of provision' may prove more appropriate.

NOTES

The research described in this article has been supported by the Joseph Rowntree Memorial Trust as part of a programme on 'The Future of Work'.

The source of the UK time budget material described in Tables 2 and 3 are discussed in J. Gershuny and S. Jones, 'The Changing Work/Leisure Balance in Britain, 1961–1984', *Sociological Review Monograph 33*, Jan. 1987; the multinational comparative material illustrated in Figures 1 and 2 is described in detail in *Time Use in Seven Countries, 1961 to 1984*, J. Gershuny and S. Jones, University of Bath, mimeo, 1986 (105 pp); and a briefer outline of the multinational results is contained in 'Time Use, Technology and the Future of Work', *Journal of the Market Research Society*, Vol. 28, No. 4, 1986.

Reflections About Some Basic Concepts for Services Economics

by

Gonzales d'Alcantara

This article focuses on the possibilities of inserting new concepts in the spaces left in the modern micro-economic framework in order to allow for an appropriate and specific treatment of services. Starting from micro-economic theory in a nutshell and using this framework as a reference, the author points to six of its characteristics wherein services have to be introduced. Three essential functions of services are then developed, which provide a bridge between the economics of services and other disciplines such as psychology, sociology and cultural anthropology.

INTRODUCTION

While the post-industrialised economies are increasingly turning into service economies, most of our mental schemes have been shaped to manage object-economies. Our economic theories are based on an objectal conception of human needs and activities. The essence of services however does not concern objects, but rather relationships, socialisation, organisation, knowledge. Etymologically, '*servire*: to be someone's slave', and '*inservire*: to be useful to someone', point to the inter-individual relationship. We also have to include relationships between the individual and the organisation and between organisations. On this basis we try to summarise some basic concepts for an appropriate approach of services economics.

First, we show that an economic theory of services requires the extension of the main concepts of traditional micro-economic theory. The essence of services involves agents, activities and relationships as opposed to objects. We show how the undifferentiated goods and services of the Competitive Equilibrium model lead to a list of questions about relationships which may be considered as forming the basis for the field of service economics.

Six issues are considered which introduce services on top of the Competitive Equilibrium set-up:

- information production and consumption processes such as auction mechanisms or planning and rationing mechanisms are necessary to make the price system work;
- in order to work out a Competitive Equilibrium, agents need to

communicate, meet, contract, compare available alternatives; they need to produce and consume relationships;
- the establishment, distribution and protection of initial endowments require economic resources;
- socialisation activities imply that individual and social decision-makers have strongly interdependent preferences, structures and dynamics;
- invention, innovation and diffusion of new technologies produce economies of scale and life-cycle dynamics in all production, consumption and organisational processes and in services themselves;
- the identity preservation of goods, firms, consumers and other institutions requires maintenance and repair activities.

Second, it is essential to identify the three essential functions of services which will allow us to determine a general methodology for the study of services. These three functions are access, regulation and foundation:

- being in or establishing relationships means having or producing *access* to commodities or agents;
- production of access is based on *regulation* of repetition, maintenance and destruction of relationships;
- regulation of access is a repetitive process organised on the original *foundation* of identity and differentiation which condition relationships.

Third, we provide the overall structure for the detailed analysis of the regulation function of services. Services have to be seen as regulatory systems.

A more detailed analysis of regulation mechanisms included in services shows that there are close complementarity and substitution relationships between different forms of regulation such as cultural, political or economic regulation mechanisms. The economic theory of regulation indicates where the market clearing or flexible price regulation is valid and why its applicability may be limited. There are conditions where one uses non-market clearing or fixed price and rationing regulation schemes. Similarly there are conditions where hierarchical organisations provide the framework for managing complex relationships between agents. Finally one also has non-economic regulation mechanisms embodied in language and culture in general.

ECONOMIC THEORY IN A NUTSHELL

Let us start from the Competitive Equilibrium model which is used as an implicit or explicit reference in most policy-oriented discussions on productivity and competitiveness. There is no dominant and well-established theory of services. Economic theory deals with 'goods and services' without making any fundamental distinction. Let us provisionally call them 'commodities'.

We first examine an economy in the traditional and most general theoretical economic set-up and then check how services fit or do not fit into the picture.

An economy is defined by distinguishing the following basic elements which have to be considered as given *a priori*:

(i) r commodities : $h = 1, r$

(ii) n firms : $j = 1, n$ defined by their production set $Y_j \subset \mathcal{R}^r$; y_j is the net production vector of firm j; y is > 0 if an output and < 0 if an input.

(iii) m consumers : $i = 1, m$ defined by their consumption set $X_i \subset \mathcal{R}^r$, their utility function $u_i(x) : X_i \to \mathcal{R}$, their initial endowments vector $w_i \, \varepsilon \, \mathcal{R}_i^r$ and a vector $\Theta_i = [\Theta_{i1} \cdots \Theta_{in}]$ where Θ_{ij} indicate the share consumer i holds in firm j; we have $\Sigma_i \Theta_{ij} = 1$ for $\forall j$; x_{ih} is > 0 if a consumption and < 0 if supply of labour.

Economic Theory following Arrow and Debreu [1954] defines a 'Competitive Equilibrium' (C.E.) as a triplet [p*, y*, x*] with p* > 0, x*=[x$_i^*$, ... x$_m^*$] and y*=[y*, ... y$_n^*$] which satisfy

(iv) the resources-uses balance
$$-\Sigma_j y_j^* + \Sigma_i x_i^* \leq \Sigma_i w_i ;$$

(v) the profit maximisation under the production possibility constraint
$$\forall j : y_j^* \, \varepsilon \, Y_j \text{ and } \not\exists y_j^o \, \varepsilon \, Y_j \text{ s.t. } p^* y_j^o > p^* y_j^* ;$$

(vi) the utility maximisation under the budget constraint
$$\forall i : x_i^* \text{ maximizes } u_i(x_i)$$
in the set $\{x_i \, \varepsilon \, X_i | p^* x_i \leq p^* w_i + \Sigma_j \Theta_{ij} p^* y_j^* \}$.

We can partition consumers and firms into countries and introduce an exchange rate parameter differentiating country currencies without loss of generality.

We know from economic theory that under classical assumptions (convexity of each Y_j and X_i and quasi concavity of each u_i) there *exists* a Competitive Equilibrium (CE) and that this C.E. is Pareto optimal if all u are strictly increasing. This means that there exists a price vector such that, knowing the price vector and his own characteristics, each agent is able to compute his decisions x$_i^*$ and y$_j^*$ and the resulting actions are *compatible* and *optimal* in the sense that one could not improve any agent without harming at least one other.

This set-up has been extended to take into account a large number of problems:

(vii) each agent has a *time horizon* covering T periods t by extending the space of goods and endowments over r x T; the price vector p* now includes the future prices of all future markets;

(viii) one introduces *uncertainty* by introducing a finite set of states of nature W_s with $s = 1, \ldots S$ which appear independently of any human action and extending the space of goods and endowments over r x T x S. The utility functions and the production functions become weighted by probability measures and can be interpreted as state-dependent functions. The price vector p* can now be interpreted as insurance premiums. $p*_{hts}$ is the price of good h in market t conditioned on the occurrence of state s.

These extensions of the model do not modify the essence of the basic concepts introduced under (i), (ii), (iii).

THE IMPLICITNESS OF SERVICES IN THE C.E. MODEL

The C.E. model has been generalised to take into account such problems as externalities, non-convexities, public goods, non-competitive structure of the economy or incomplete markets. A general approach for services has not yet been proposed. While this Pareto Optimal Competitive Equilibrium is an implicit or explicit reference in most policy-oriented discussions on efficiency and effectivity, a large part of services cannot be interpreted within the usual C.E. framework and certainly cannot be considered as simply specific elements of the vector x in the range of h. We develop six characteristics of this model which show this.

1. The theory of competitive equilibrium, which ensures efficiency, does not say by whom the *equilibrium price* vector p* has to be *decided* on and how it has to be *reached*. Will it be decided on by a Walrasian Auctioneer, or a Central Planning Bureau or some monopolistic price leader? The C.E. mechanism as such requires an additional 'service' to be made operational. One needs to introduce a privileged agent, the centre, which will process the *information* needed to determine prices. The competitive equilibrium is consistent with decentralised decision-making, where all information transfers take place through prices on condition that these prices are decided on in a consistent way, which implies using economic resources for the organisation of a process: one central or many interrelated market places (with auction mechanisms), one central or many inter-related planning offices (with planning or rationing mechanisms). In other words, the C.E. requires a *regulation* process which implies a preference revelation activity requiring economic resources. These activities characterise service activities.

2. The theory of competitive equilibrium does not introduce an explicit description of how the economic agents communicate, meet, contract, and better compare available alternatives in terms of utility, profit or technology. In other words, it does not explain how the *relationships between the agents* are established, repeated over time or interrupted.

Resources are needed for the processing of contracts, of transaction activities and of information exchanges. All these activities are typical service activities.

The inter-relationships between firms, and between firms, workers and consumers require contractual and cultural socialisation processes which are typically provided in service activities.

Purchasing policies, relationships with actual and potential clients and marketing services are not included in the C.E. model unless they can be regarded as integral parts of the goods. In that case they are not regarded specifically as services.

3. The theory of the competitive equilibrium determines neither how *the endowments* of the agents are *established* and *distributed* nor how they are *protected*. In practice, endowments mean that the agents have *access* to goods and resources. This access is not given naturally but is the result of an institutional, political or even military activity which requires resources. The history of wars and violence clearly shows up to what point the use of important economic resources have been justified in order to enable collectives to survive internally and externally. We need the services of lawyers, diplomatic agents, military experts to produce the stability and dynamics of the endowments.

4. The fourth characteristic results from the fact that modern research on the *structure and dynamics of preferences* could not reject the hypothesis that the consumers' preference structure is not given exogeneously but is signficantly influenced by the firms or by other consumers. The structure and evolution of preferences result from the consumers' socialisation process. The objects are identified as consumables because they are integrated in cultural systems. Needs are determined by cultural patterns. But cultural patterns are not at all independent from the economic activities, from the goods consumed and from the available technologies. There is a whole range of educational services, information services, media services and cultural services, the main function of which is to shape and keep preferences in a collectively consistent range.

5. The fifth characteristic is related to the similar fact that *technologies* are not exogeneously given, but result from the invention, innovation and diffusion processes which are partly endogeneous to the economic system. They result from the agents' decision-making and not from the state of nature. Another way of looking at this is to acknowledge that in a 'competitive' equilibrium nothing is said about the process of competition or co-operation which can lead to the competitive state. Because of the acceleration of technical progress, economists now recognise that competition is not only 'price-competition' as is implied by the C.E. model, but also 'non-price competition and/or co-operation' for the development of economies of scale and improvements in production technologies (process innovation), consumption technologies (product innovation) and organisational or management technologies.

Schumpeterian economics show how competition relies on the speed of *differentiation* (invention, innovation)on the one hand and on the speed of *imitation* (diffusion) on the other hand. This is what Research and Development services produce. One knows how crucial these activities are in determining *market structures* and therefore of economic regulation modes. This is typically the case when company monopolies result from competition over technological standards in infrastructures for communication networks or languages for communication services.

6. C.E. starts from goods, firms and consumers, which exist and constitute stable references. Nothing is more illusory than perfect identity preservation. Goods, firms and consumers not only have a life-cycle but their identity during the life-cycle is not stable. These life-cycles have an initial point of foundation. The uncertainty and risk related to their survival require a large amount of services.

These may be maintenance services, services to restore or reconstitute commodities, firms or consumers. The instability of commodities, firms or consumers is revealed by symptoms of dysfunctioning, such as defect, pollution, conflicts, failures and illness at many levels. This requires preventive and curative service activity before the C.E. game can start! Services have to restore the integrity and health of the environment, private and public companies and consumers.

A crucial general point is that the internal nature of services, conceived as the activities establishing the relationships, requires appropriate internal and external regulation. This regulation needs to be made explicit in the C.E. model while it interacts with the C.E. mechanism itself.

TOWARDS A FUNCTIONAL DEFINITION OF SERVICES

At present, the best generally admitted definition of services among economists is 'the content of all economic transactions which are not classifed as goods'. This definition covers both market and non-market (public sector and non-profit) services, both official and non-official and non-official (black, underground) services, and both paid and unpaid (domestic, do-it-yourself) services. Services may be provided by individuals (human capital), by organisations (social capital) or by durable goods (consumer durables accumulated, equipment goods, nature as a capital). Services may be primary, intermediary (for the use of enterprises) or final (for the use of the household or government sector). Services may be produced and consumed simultaneously or consumed after a lapse of time (stored in durable goods like a song festival on a videotape), *in situ* or at a distance (via communication infrastructure). Services can be more or less non-material, permanent, reversible, appropriable . . . But these categories do not tell us what is the essential nature and structure of a relationship, what exactly is produced, consumed and distributed. We are mainly interested in the definition of the output and the process rather than the inputs of services.

To identify the specific nature of *services*, as opposed to goods, we start from the concept of 'being in relationship', as opposed to 'being an object'.

An *object* is essentially the result of a separation, a difference, a frontier between the object itself and the subject or another object. The enacting of a relationship is essentially a linking together of diffferent subjects or objects and subjects. Service economies require a theory of relationships between the elements of the economic system.

A *relationship* implies two poles: each pole is precisely one of the elements of the C.E. framwork: commodities, consumers and firms, i.e., objects and agents. A service seen as a relationship can be systematised by three functions:

1. The function of *access* establishes the existence of the relationship itself: distribution and transport services establish the relationship between agents and objects; communication services establish the relationship between agents (individual or sub-organisations).

The access function of services can be described using graph theoretical tools. Graph theory will allow us to describe complex systems of access. This may involve simplifying the structure, by keeping only relationships essential to the nature of the internal interdependence, and by isolating sub-systems or microsystems which may have interesting autonomous properties due to internal interdependence, and which enter into relation with other sub- or microsystems. Furthermore, access services are a matter of engineering and are studied in hard economic disciplines such as transport economics, queuing theory, networking theory, etc.

2. The function of *regulation* establishes the need for a balance between the two poles of a relationship. This produces the conditions for the establishment, the repetition or the permanence of the relationship without interruption occurring whether because the relationship is breaking; because one of the poles is destroyed; because the two poles merge, or because one absorbs the other.

Regulation deals with the uncertainty and the risk of interruption of the relationship. In addition, there are many modes of regulation. They can be classified as

- *cultural* modes of regualtion through habits and language which determine socialisation processes;
- *economic* modes of regulation mainly market clearing (flexible prices) or non-market clearing (rigid prices, rationing) regulation. A large part of service productivity is related to efficient and effective regulation in connection with *price and non-price competition* and to *co-operation;*
- *political* modes of regulation including regulation by hierarchical organisations and all forms of state regulation by legal or military means.

Productive regulation is able to reproduce a well-identified relationship between agents, so as to control the inner structure of the relationship and to reproduce the social and economic identity of individuals and groups through a natural life cycle. This applies to administrative, political (procedures), religious (rituals) or psychological (therapeutic processes) services, as soon as the service has been sufficiently well identified and standardised to be statistically observable.

Regulation includes the control of conflictual relationships and the various forms of violence which they can generate at the physical (injuries), economic (unfair competition), political (wars), social (exclusion) and symbolic (dominance) level.

The optimal choice and development of appropriate regulation mechanisms is a crucial issue in the improving of productivity and requires an inventory of what happens to relationships in the absence of regulation:

- ineffective or inefficient production or consumption of objects, access, regulation
- number and nature of cases of dysfunctioning health: illness, premature death
- number and nature of cases of psychological dysfunction: complaints, internment or confinement in psychiatric institutions
- number and nature of acts which fail, accidents on the road and at work, fires
- number and nature of infringements of laws and rules, robberies, acts of vandalism, rapes, crimes, murders, suicides, wars

Regulation has results in terms of improvement of disequilibrium signals, dysfunctional symptoms or counterproductivity indicators which express the outcome of potential conflicts rooted in relationships. It should also reduce uncertainty about the various forms of violence.

3. The function of *foundation* is to establish creative conditions for the relationships' existence in space and time. It contributes to the dynamics of human relationships by ensuring a 'flow' of creative 'ruptures' which form the basis of the transformation of culture and the economy under the pressure of disequilibria or in crises. It generates new forms of differentiation through inventive entrepreneurship, artistic creation and scientific discovery. It relies on the human individual, who is an open system of awareness. This function needs to be assumed to be the source of human creativity revealed by technological change, and to be the purpose of the economic system revealed by preference orderings. It determines the initial point of any life cycle of a product in service. This point includes the concept of invention of the Schumpeterian trilogy. Inventions qualify historical discoveries or discontinuities which make room for new scientific and social paradigms which affect the processes of production, consumption and distribution of objects and relationships. Inventions are by definition subject to uncertainty and at most, formalised through subjective probabilities. Within a paradigm we could also use the term of invention when small discontinuities of the differentiated form of service are only subjectively probable.

The output of services may be analysed in terms of access, regulation and foundation processes. We study the functional components of services and not a classification or partition of services. As such, services may remain internal to the industrial sector or be externalised: in both cases the productivitiy criterion will be similar. The point of introducing these criteria is not to use them to partition the services into three classes, but rather to characterise the specific components within a service activity or service technology. For example, health care services help to restore physical integrity but also to regulate relationships when illnesses can be interpreted as somatic symptoms of malfunctioning interindividual relationships. Where education is concerned, the learning of languages provides an access to natural communication with other individuals, but also operates a regulation of the interindividual relationship and of the socialisation process of individuals while integrating them into reference groups.

The improvement of productivity in the services will thus be seen as the achievement of more efficient (minimal inputs) and more effective (best alternative outputs) access, regulation and foundation processes.

TOWARDS A GENERAL THEORY OF REGULATION

It should be clear by now that there can be no valid theory of services which does not consider regulation mechanisms as outputs to be produced under productive conditions, since regulation is integral to the concept of service or relationship. The internal efficiency and effectiveness of the service essentially depends on an external regulation mechanism which controls the service performance at any stage in its life cycle and in each of its components (access, internal regulation, foundation). Economists are used to considering monetary regulation mechanisms and they distinguish between market and administered (non-market) monetary regulations.

We need to investigate the properties of the regulation mechanisms, the market regulation which defines market places, specifies rules, barriers (to entry, contingents), protections (patents, antitrust), the administered procedures (legal procedures, sanctions) and the non-economic regulation mechanisms.

In addition to monetary market and non-market monetary mechanisms one has to acknowledge the existence of other non-monetary regulation mechanisms which are mainly cultural differentiation mechanisms (habitus), linguistic differentiation as described, e.g., by Bourdieux [1982] and the legal and repressive order of the state as developed, e.g., by Enriques [1983].

The crucial contribution from economic research in this field is that economics make it quite explicit that regulation mechanisms presuppose information structures. In order to understand regulation mechanisms, it is essential to know what information the different agents possess when making their decisions and in what way they dynamically update their information sets with new information. Different information structures require different regulation mechanisms. This problem is just as central on the micro-economic as on the macro-economic level, because for each agent it is important to know how the information gained from other agents should be interpreted, as he or she has to base decisions on this information. At the same time, at the macro-economic level this problem is of crucial importance because wrong mechanisms can lead to long-lasting disequilibria which will affect all agents through the cultural, political, social and finally the economic (investment, fiscal) climate.

REFERENCES

d'Alcantara, G., 1987 'From Service Productivity to Service Regulation and Regulating Service', *Service Industries Journal,* Vol.7, No.2.

Andersen, T.M., 1985 *Allocation under differential information – flexible and fixed prices,* doctoral thesis presented at the Catholic University of Louvain.

Arrow, K.J. and G. Debreu, 1954, 'Existence of an Equilibrium for a Comptitive Economy', *Econometrica,* Vol.22.

Bourdieux, P., 1982, *Ce que parler veut dire* (L'économie des échanges linguistiques), Paris: Fayard.

Enriques, E., 1983, *De la horde à l'état. Essai de psychanalyse du lien social,* Paris: Gallimard.

Girard, R., 1978, *Des choses cachées depuis la fondation du monde,* recherches avec J.M. Oughourlian et G. Lefort, Paris: Editions Bernard Grasset.

Harsanyi, J., 1977, *Rational Behaviour and Bargaining Equilibrium in Games and Social Situations,* Cambridge: University Press.

Selten, R., 1985, *Bureaucratic Budget Bargaining as a Game of Incomplete Information,* University of Bonn.

Services Markets and the Economics of Social Interaction

by

Pieter Tordoir

There is symbolically transmitted personal and cultural meaning involved in interpersonal service transactions, for which economic explanation has to account. Language, symbols and interpretations are an important context for many 'rational' services. The market-dynamics of many advanced services in the post-industrial economy result from rational use of these symbols and interpretations in the course of strategic economic interaction. 'Strategic services' expand into the social sphere of informal, 'communicative' action (the process of rationalisation). In order to account for these aspects, a platform for interdisciplinary services-research has to be created. We can draw in this respect upon ideas of Habermas.

INTRODUCTION

How far are the various strands of contemporary economics leading towards a better understanding of services dynamics? Regarding economic research on services, economists can be divided into three camps; those who do not (yet) recognise the services as an important field for research and theory-development, those who have worked on the subject and are able to encapsulate it within a pre-existing theoretical framework without changing the latter, and finally those who adapt theory and concepts, confronting new information on services and the need for new methods of investigation and interpretation of services dynamics. These three camps intersect the dividing lines between the vested doctrines of economic theory and research practices. Researchers who are known for their innovative ideas can be very conservative when faced with services dynamics. Among the critical or neo-Marxian economists, for example, all three camps are represented (compare the writings on services of Walker [1985], Lipietz [1983] and Gadrey [1985-6]). Clearly, the recognition and valuation of service activities are not a monopoly of any of the research doctrines.

Those economists who develop a theoretical and conceptual framework for investigation and explanation of services all encounter the same problems, irrespective of their strand. In short, these problems are of a threefold nature. First, there is the well-known problem of intangibility of services, leading to a disutility of common yardsticks for objectivation and quantification of production-technique, output and consumption. Second, there is a problem in case the services can only be evaluated within a social and institutional context [Moulaert, 1986$_a$, 1986$_b$, de Swaan, 1986]. A third problem is encountered if the value and the function of a service cannot be estimated without any consideration of the personality and the personal life-world (*Lebenswelt* in the Heideggerian sense) of the participants involved in a service-transaction. Of course these three problems have much in common. But as yet only the first problem of intangibility is fully recognised by economists working on the field of services, the second problem much less so, and the third problem not at all.

Each of these three problems can only be tackled if the existing data of economic science are more or less transgressed. Regarding the problem of intangibility, and the problem of the social-institutional context, such a transgression implies the embodiment of qualitative concepts in the conceptual framework of economics, a de-physicalisation of the science at least to some degree. But in particular regarding the 'personality' problem, one will run aground on a common datum limiting all the current economic strands: this is the datum of objectification, of instrumental or purpose-rational human behaviour, as the latter is opposed to communicative action (analogous to the differentiation made by Habermas between *Arbeit* and *Interaktion*).

The argument here is that, depending on the kind of service and its social-institutional context, there is an important layer of communicative and symbolic interaction involved in services markets, which could be a major source for the economic dynamics of the sector. Therefore, the demarcation between subject and object could be more important than the commonly investigated demarcation between tangible and intangible economic output. Transgression of the first demarcation implying a subjectification in methods, is a most formidable task, however. It means that a methodological discussion with a long history in sociology and the hermeneutical sciences would be started in economics. Recent writings by the researchers involved in the Johns Hopkins programme on services show that the consideration of the intangibility as well as the social-institutional context of services activities is very well possible and leading towards a deepening of the theoretical framework of the discipline [Dyckman *et al.*, 1986]. Is it possible to take yet another step further, in order to reach the symbolic 'life-world' context of many services, what could we expect from such a step for the explanation of the dynamics of services markets?

One of the first questions that comes to mind is whether the existence, regarding exchanges of service, of factors and processes which cannot be grasped by the economic language is of any significance to the economic explanation of service markets.

Sociology and psychology make contributions to the understanding of almost any of the social phenomena investigated by economics, such as firm-behaviour or consumer-behaviour. The objectivation or abstraction of such complex phenomena in economic concepts is legitimated if it adds something to our general understanding. As far as service exchanges are governed by economic rationality and as far as services are scarce resources exchanged in more or less open markets, ruled by objective exchange values, the embodiment of service actitivities in 'objective' economic terms has theoretical and practical relevance. This presupposes at least two distinct spheres regarding service exchanges, one of which is a formal market-sphere where economic rational behaviour is predominant, whereas other kinds of (ir-)rational behaviour characterise the other sphere(s). The explanation of the latter could, in this rather simplistic view, be handed over to sociology, the political sciences, or the hermeneutical sciences, assumed that there are no interfering relations between the spheres.

Regarding the phenomenon of service markets in particular, however, these assumptions are anything but realistic, for at least three reasons. First, there is a large 'grey area' between pure economic rationality and pure non-economic rationality. Examples of this grey area are the services supplied or regulated by public agencies. Second, even those services most directly ruled by economic rationality are to some degree subject to non-economic influences (the assumption of pure economic rationality is, for that matter, of course as much debatable in the case of goods production and goods consumption) [Moulaert, 1986]. Finally, the lines of demarcation between the different spheres, or the different rationalities, are in constant movement. Informal service exchanges (within the family, for example) are formalised; formal markets, on the other hand, are losing trade to the informal sector [Miles, 1985]. These movements could explain much of the dynamics of particular service markets, but they cannot be fully understood by a single disciplinary language. Therefore, lack of communication between the various scientific disciplines and methods must be avoided. Interdisciplinary communication and research, however, are only possible if the various languages are adapted in order to create a platform for mutual understanding. The work of Jürgen Habermas contains valuable ideas on how to proceed.

Habermas conceives social reality as consisting of some distinct subsystems (the technological-economical subsystem, the political sub-system, the family, for example) set in a global social-institutional framework. In his *Technologie und Wissenschaft als 'Ideologie'* [1968] he makes a distinction between social subsystems dominated by goal-oriented rational action on the one hand and social subsystems characterised by symbolically transmitted or communicative interaction on the other. As I argued above, such a distinction could be made within the field of service exchanges although the matter is not as simple as that. The value of Habermas's idea lies rather in his consideration of the movements of the lines of demarcation between the subsystems, in particular the enlargement of the field of goal-rational action at the cost of communicative interaction (Habermas, 1963). In order to develop this theory of the process of rationalisation, he created a conceptual language which could help us constructing a platform for interdisciplinary services research.

ECONOMIC RATIONALITY AND STRATEGIC INTERACTION

We could state that the problem of the intangibility and therefore the unmeasurability of services is a nuisance to be overcome; in so far as service markets are ruled by economic rationality, the subject is open to economic investigation. Following the arguments raised by Coppieters [1986] and Tordoir [1986], this rationality can relate to services used as 'technical' tools for production or for consumption, or it can relate to regulatory services. Translated in concepts used by Habermas: instrumental services, and strategic services. Instrumental services function in some distinctive production-technique or consumption-technique. Examples of these services are transport, repair, retailing or training. Strategic services on the other hand, relate to strategic behaviour of individuals or of organisations: the influencing of social interaction. They can take the form of negotiation (ex trade), or power-backed regulation (ex bureaucratic management),or of opinon-inducement (ex marketing). Some services, such as many of the media-services, are characterised by a mixture of instrumental and strategic purposes. Finally, services can be instrumental in the course of strategic interaction, as is the case with market research or management consultancy. Both kinds of services can be exchanged in an open market environment, as well as in a bureaucratic or in a co-operative environment. Perhaps it is somewhat odd to think of exchanges regarding strategic services; the concept of a game, or a 'visible hand', is more appropriate in pointing out their character. Chandler's concept of a 'visible hand' ruling the corporate economy [1977], and Bell's concept of a cybernetic society [1973] both point to this character of strategic services. Both authors give impressive accounts of the dynamics of these activities, which are the hallmark of a new kind of rationality and functionality, the control and regulation of complex social-economic systems. Strategic services as defined above are rational in an economic sense if they are functional for the development and maintenance of the whole and parts of the economic-technological subsystem in society, in the terms of Habermas. As such, however, they are framed in a global social-institutional context [Habermas, 1968; Moulaert, 1986a, Gadrey 1985]. Naturally, instrumental services are as well framed in such a context (open market, regulated market, bureaucratic organisation). But the presence of this context is made more explicit regarding strategic services, if only because social interaction and social regulation are involved.

How can the social-institutional context of services, in particular strategic services, be considered and accounted for by economic or social-functionalistic conceptualisations? Both Moulaert and Gadrey, economists by profession, remain in a functionalistic and catascopic perspective when accounting for the social and institutional framework, or character, of services. In his article, Moulaert emphasises the institutional environment of services in productive systems, whereas Gadrey gives an account of the social context of the final consumption of services.Like Habermas, Moulaert is worried about the encapsulation of this context by pure and relentless economic rationality. Unlike Habermas, however, he considers the context in terms of functional categories and 'agents'. Habermas, however, is, in the sociological tradition set by Weber (1968), averse to a pure functionalistic perspective, for which he heavily attacks Marxist scholars. If we explain the social-institutional character and environment of services in pure functionalistic terms, we forget the aspects of legitimacy, meaning and personal interpretation present in each interpersonal service exchange and its social context. We tend to forget that each exchange of pure services, or of strategic services, involves symbols, or language. For the valuation of 'rational' services we need to consider personal meaning and language as well as social-economic functions and institutions. If we do not do so, we assume that the former is fully encapsulated by the latter: we would be living in the de-personalised world sketched by Baudrillard [1970]. In my opinion, we cannot assume that the sphere of instrumental and strategic services is fully dominated by economic rationality. Moreover, we cannot assume that the social context of this sphere is a matter of objective functions.

SERVICES AND COMMUNICATIVE INTERACTION

Often the value of a service for a consumer is related to the personality of the producer of the service. The value I gave to the courses in university was 40 per cent determined by sympathy felt for the teachers, 40 per cent by the symbolic value I gave to the subject and 20 per cent at most by rational calculation. Regarding my daily shopping I am willing to pay 20 per cent extra in order to maintain a pleasant contact with the local small retailers, avoiding the efficiency of supermarkets. In doing so, I join half of the population of Amsterdam, according to research done by Jansen [1982]. Other aspects in the valuation of services which cannot be calculated are the patterns of social legitimacy and symbolic meaning. Personal services imply that we deal with other persons; we behave according to a great many cultural rules and personal rules. To pay for a service is for example in many occasions 'not done': you repay with a service, or with a good of symbolic value for both parties in the exchange. Perhaps more than 90 per cent of the service market is a barter-market; most services are exchanges within a family or a circle of friendly people.

The result of a service, or the consumption-value, is often of less interest to the consumer as is the value of the interpersonal interaction itself. Why do we enjoy our work? Relations with others count as much as results and salaries. Again, these symbolic and personal valuations could apply as well to exchanges of goods; however, regarding goods the phenomenon is rather marginal; the production of goods is almost always a matter of pure economic rationality.

Naturally, these phenomena are characteristic of what Habermas calls the social subsystems ruled by communicative interaction. The question here is whether there are relations between the services-sphere of communicative interaction and the sphere of economic-rational action;

relations for which economic explanation has to give some account.

In the first place, both the 'communicative sphere' and the economic-rational sphere are placed in the same global social-institutional context. However, we have to add the cultural dimension to this global context. To deny the existence of the cultural environment of services (social tradition, national language, and other heritages) would severely limit the explanation of the national dynamics and economic geography of formal service markets.

In the second place, an increasing part of the subsystem or sphere of communicative interaction is subject to a process of rationalisation. Communicative services are transformed into instrumental services and strategic services. Formal markets and bureaucracies replace informal services barter. The Dutch sociologist Achterhuis gives an impressive account of this process regarding what he calls the market for well-being and happiness [Achterhuis, 1979]. In other words, the economic-rational sphere is expanding at the cost of the communcative sphere; in particular, it is the strategic service which is at the frontier zone in this movement.

Finally, a layer of communicative, symbolic interaction is existent within even the most rationally produced services. The 'looping' of fashionable concepts is perhaps one of the main sources for the dynamics of the consultancy-sector. Strategic management, for example, is 'in' today, as a concept and a symbol of modernity. Not many know what it stands for, hence, the market for strategic management-consultants is booming. And what to think about concepts such as 'logistics', 'innovation'? Baudrillard's analysis of the processes of self-reference and symbolic differentiation in the case of the media-services is a good example of how service markets grow and collapse [Baudrillard, 1970]. Symbols and interpretations are not only the medium for many of the advanced producer services, they are the main game as well. We can think of 'concept-cycles' (analogous to product-cycles) and concept-families explaining the market dynamics of these services. As far as such conceptual games are ruled by economic purposes, by strategic intentions, there is need for economic explanation of social, symbolic interaction.

REFERENCES

Achterhuis, H. 1980, *De Markt van Welzijn en Geluk*. Meppel: Boom.

Baudrillard, J., 1970, *La Société de Consommation* Paris: Grasset.

Bell, D., 1973, *The Coming of the Postindustrial Society*. New York: Basic Books.

Chandler, A.D., 1977, *The Visible Hand. The Managerial Revolution in American Business*. Cambridge, MA: Harvard University Press.

Coppieters, P., 1986, 'On the Classification of Services. Reflexions from the Belgian Experience', in Dyckman, J.D., *et al.*, *The Functions of Services*, op. cit.

Dyckman, J.D., *et al.*, 1986, *The Functions of Services and the Theoretical Approach to National and International Classifications*. Lille: Johns Hopkins European Center for Regional Planning and Research.

Gadrey, J., 1986, *Les Principaux Courants d'Analyse de la Croissance des Services dans les Economies Developpées*. Paper, U.F.R. de Sciences Economiques, Université de Lille I.

Gadrey, J., 1985, *Sur L'Importance de L'Analyse des Besoins de Services*. Paper, U.F.R. des Sciences Economiques, Université de Lille I.

Habermas, J, 1968, *Techniek und Wissenschaft als 'Ideologie'*. Frankfurt: Suhrkamp Verlag.

Habermas, J., 1963, *Theorie und Praxis*. Neuwied: Herman Luchterhand.

Jansen, A.C.M., 1982, *Ondernemers in Camperstraat en Omgeving*. EGI-paper no XXI, Faculty of Economics, University of Amsterdam.

Lipietz, A., 1977, *Le Capital et son Espace* (1983 ed.) Paris: Maspiro.

Miles, I., 1985, 'The New Postindustrial State', in *Futures*, Vol.17, No.6.

Moulaert, F., 1986, 'Une Approche Fonctionelle de la Classification des Activités Economique', in Dyckman, J.D., *et al., The Functions of Services*, op. cit.

Moulaert, F., P.P. Tordoir, and J.D. Dyckman, 1986, *The International Division of Services (IDS)* Paper presented at the 33rd North American Meetings of the RSA, Columbus (Ohio).

Tordoir, P.P., 1986, 'The Significance of Services and Classifications of Services' in Dyckman, J.D., *et al., The Functions of Services*, op. cit.

de Swaan, A., 1986, 'Werkloosheid als Verkwisting', in *Intermediair*, Vol.22, No.5.

Walker, R.A., 1985, 'Is there a Service Economy? The Changing Capitalist Division of Labor', in *Science & Society*, Vol.XLIX, No.1.

Weber, M., 1968, *Economy and Society. An Outline of Interpretative Sociology*. Bedminster Press (transl. from the German.)

Development of the Service Sector: A Critical Survey of Macro-economic Models

by

Piet Coppieters

The slow-down in the economic growth and the rise in unemployment have revived the discussion about the opportunities for growth through the development of the service sector. This article reviews what models tell us about the mechanism of the development of the service industries. An attempt is made to specify the relative importance of demand and supply aspects of the service economy and to indicate the black holes in our knowledge.

INTRODUCTION

Every school of economic thought has searched for the causes of wealth and progress and formulated answers to the question: which sectors add most to economic growth? By the physiocrats the slogan *Nil solidum, nisi solum* (nothing solid except ground) was in force, while the classical economists and Marx believed in industry as the basis of economic development and growth. At the end of the nineteenth century marginalism became the mainstream thought in economic analysis and the question disappeared from the economic research agenda. But during the great depression the problem was raised again as can be seen from the following quotation [Fisher, 1933: 379]:

> In popular discussion of the depression to-day, it is commonly alleged that because 'the problem of production has been solved – we live in a world of potential plenty – the fault must lie in the process of distribution. The convincing answer to this theory is that it confuses technical and economic problems of production . . . .
>
> The practical solution of the economic problems of production is always being complicated by changes in the character and relative importance of the goods whose production it is desirable to organise.

The 'goods' which Fisher thought to be desirable to organise were

> . . . . facilities for travel, amusements of various kinds, personal and intangible services, flowers, music, art, literature, science, philosophy and the like. [Fisher, 1933: 380]

The longer the present economic crisis lasts the more one hears the question: which sectors should be stimulated by a recovery policy?

Tinbergen [1980: 35] answers:

> Along with an increase in manufacturing activity – requiring, by the way, retraining workers concurrently with receiving unemployment benefits – we have to expand the services sector. Among the various subsectors involved that of research deserves special attention.

While it is clear that employment in services now dominates in the economy of developed countries, scholars disagree as to the role of the services in the economy. Some feel that the growth of employment in services is only due to low productivity, while others argue that services are already the driving force in development economics and will be the engine of economic renovation. The first group attaches too great an importance to the role of supply and to the rate of exchange between goods and services. The latter looks only to the demand-side and neglects the interactions between both demand and supply.

This article presents a survey of macro-economic models explaining the change in economic structure. The purpose is to evaluate if these models pay attention to the different facets of the process and if one can learn something from the model world to answer Tinbergen's question. The models can be divided into three sets: demand-supply interaction models. A section is devoted to each of the three types. A fourth section contains the general conclusions.

TAYLOR'S DEVELOPMENT PATTERNS – MODEL

Taylor [1969] developed a three-sector growth model with the following characteristics:

Steady Domar-type economic growth

$I = sY$ and $Y = vI$

with I : investment s : savings rate
Y: income v: marginal output-capital
                                ratio

Only the industry sector produces investment goods.
Government expenditure (G) and consumption (C) depend on Income:

$C_i = C_i (Y)$
with i : p (primary, m (manufacturing)
and s (services)

$$G_i = a_i G \text{ with } \sum_{i=1}^{3} a_i = 1$$

Gross sector outputs are given by

$$\begin{bmatrix} X_m \\ X_p \\ X_s \end{bmatrix} = (I-A)^{-1} \begin{bmatrix} C_m^h + I + G_m + E_m \\ C_p^h + G_p + E_p \\ C_s + G_s \end{bmatrix} - \begin{bmatrix} M_{int} \\ 0 \\ 0 \end{bmatrix}$$

with A   : input-output matrix
     X   : sector outputs
     E   : exports
     M_{int} : import of intermediate goods

E_p are treated as a residual of foreign exchange to give balance-of-trade equilibrium:

$$E_p = M_{cons} + M_{int} + M_{cap} - E_m$$

The right hand variables in the balance-trade equation depend on income (Y) and population (N):

$$E_m = E_m (Y,N) \qquad\qquad M_{int} = M_{int}(Y,N)$$

$$M_{cons} = M_{cons}(Y,N) \qquad\qquad M_{cap} = M_{cap}(Y,N)$$

The solution is obtained as follows [Taylor, 1969, : 222]:

> One starts with a level on income, and derives levels of consumption, investment and government expenditure. The distribution between consumption and investment goods produced by domestic industry and imports of these goods also depends on Y, as do levels of industrial and primary exports. Once all these final demand items are computed, gross output and value added by sectors follow from the input-output relationships.

The model described above is a simple input-output general equilibrium model which provides insights into the 'stylised facts of structural change', which are known from the study of Clark [1957], Chenery [1960], Chenery and Taylor [1968], Chenery and Syrguin [1975] and Fourastié [1949]. From the functional form of the regression equation to estimate the model equations it is evident that the level of final demand is seen as the dominant factor in 'causing' structural change:

$$\ln x = a + b \ln y + c (\ln y)^2 + d \ln N.$$

The interesting feature of this equation is the quadratic terms which allows income elasticity to vary with the income level. The elasticity is equal to $b + 2c \ln y$ and its value is decreasing or increasing respectively according as $c < 0$ or $c > 0$.

The model tells us little about the impact of demand because demand is completely exogeneous and services are seen as non-tradables (see the final-demand vector). In the actual context of developed economies one should at least extend the final-demand vector with an E_s and M_s component. The model does not allow for changes in the A-matrix: no account is taken of the evolution and shifts in intermediate demand.

THE UNBALANCED GROWTH MODEL

Baumol [1967] developed a simple macro-economic model to evaluate the implications of sectoral differences in productivity for the relative proportion of these sectors in GNP and for the growth of GNP itself. We first give the essential relationships of the model and resume the conclusions derived from it by Baumol. In the second part of this section we discuss features of the model and evaluate the conclusions drawn from it.

The model

Assume a two-sector economy in which labour is the only input and labour productivity is constant in sector 1 and exponentially rising in sector 2. Wages in both sectors are equal to the marginal product in sector 2.
If X_{1t} = output for sector 1 (non-progressive sector) at time t
  X_{2t} = output for sector 2 (progressive sector at time t
  and W_t = wage per unit of labour at time t
the model's equations are:

$$X_{1t} = a \, L_{1t}$$

$$X_{2t} = b \, L_{2t} \cdot e^{rt} \qquad \text{with r : constant compound rate of}$$
$$\text{productivity growth}$$

$$W_t = W_o \cdot e^{rt}$$

$$L_t = L_{1t} + L_{2t} \qquad \text{with } L_t : \text{total employment at time t}$$

One can now derive the following properties of such a system:
1. If prices are proportionate to costs, the price per unit of output (P_{1t}) will rise without limit while P_{2t} will remain constant. One can easily prove that:

$$\frac{P_{1t}}{P_{2t}} = \frac{b \, e^{rt}}{a}$$

2. Assuming that price elasticity for both goods is one, the output ratio of the sectors becomes:

$$\frac{X_1}{X_2} = \frac{a \dfrac{L_{1t}}{L_{2t}}}{b \, e^{rt}} \qquad \frac{L_{1t}}{L_{2t}} \text{ is constant because,}$$

price elasticity = 1 assures that the relative outlays on the two goods remain constant. With t → ∞ the ratio declines towards zero.
3. If the ratio is maintained constant (e.g. through government subsidy) all labour flows to the non-progressive sector. Assume:

$$\frac{X_{1t}}{X_{2t}} = \frac{a \, L_{1t}}{b \, L_{2t} \cdot e^{rt}} = C$$

then $L_{1t} = \dfrac{L_t \cdot C \cdot e^{rt}}{1 + C\,e^{rt}}$ thus for $t \to \infty$ $L_{1t} \to L_t$

A low price inelasticity and a large income elasticity for good 2 will as well as government intervention assure a constant output ratio.

4. If the output ratio is kept constant and the growth rate of the economy will asymptotically approach zero.

Assume $L_t = L$ or total labour supply is constant and the index of output is a weighted average of the outputs of both sectors $0 = B_1 X_1 + B_2 X_2$ then Baumol proves that:

$$\dfrac{\dfrac{d\,0}{d\,t}}{0} = \dfrac{r}{1 + K\,e^{rt}} \quad \text{with } K = \text{a constant}$$

which means that the percentage rate of growth as t approaches infinity, will tend to approach zero.

Baumol associates the progressive sector with manufacturing and the non-progressive sector with the service industries, 'activities which, by their very nature, permit only sporadic increases in productivity'. Baumol concludes [1967: 421]:

> Our model tells us that manufactures are likely to continue to decline in relative costs and, unless the income elasticity of demand from manufactured goods is very large, they may absorb an ever smaller proportion of the labor force, which if it transpires, may make it more difficult for our economy to maintain its over all rate of output growth.

Evaluation of the model

The model which Baumol advances provides interesting insight into the economic events with which the real world deals. However, he paints the world in black and white. In his model he looks to reality only from the supply-side. As we see in the next section, if one introduces the demand-side the conclusions drawn from his analyses are much less straightforward. But even when we stick to the supply-side one can argue that Baumol's view (because of the single-factor assumption and the wage assumption) gives a too pessimistic impression of unbalanced growth.

Bradford [1969] demonstrated that in a two-factor economy and with not very unlikely sorts of factor complementarity, two of the conclusions no longer hold. From the production functions it is clear that the production possibility frontier is linear with slope $-a/b\,e^{rt}$, which means that the marginal rate of transformation is independent of the output ratio at any time. Property one and two depend upon this feature of the model. In the two-factor assumption a curved production possibility frontier is to be expected. 'We can no longer speak of the (marginal) cost of one commodity in terms of another without specifying precisely where on the frontier of the moment such a quantity is to be calculated'[Bradford, 1969: 301]. In this situation it is possible to produce a constant volume of X_1, while the capacity to produce X_2 continually expands.

The consequences of unbalanced growth also depend strongly on Baumol's assumption of the wage formation mechanism: wages are equal to the marginal product in the progressive sector. If, however, one starts from the competitive market solution and adopts a wage-income policy to guarantee an equivalent income to both the employee in the non-progressive sector and the employee in the progressive sector, it can be demonstrated that the relative costs of the outputs of sector 1 and sector 2 remain constant [Nonneman and De Wachter, 1976: 9]. Let:

$$\left. \begin{array}{l} W_{1t} = W_0 \\ W_{2t} = W_0\, e^{rt} \end{array} \right\} \text{ be the competitive market solution}$$

and assume a wage-income transmission mechanism by which a part of the wage W_{2t} is not paid to the employee in sector 2 (i.e. the employee is obliged to deduct a tax) but is transferred to a wage-fund from which workers in sector 1 are paid a surplus to their wage, W_0. Then the relative prices, if they are cost related, become:

$$\frac{P_{1t}}{P_{2t}} = \frac{\dfrac{W_0\, L_{1t}}{a\, L_{1t}}}{\dfrac{W_0\, e^{rt}\, L_{2t}}{b\, L_{2t}\, e^{rt}}} = \frac{b}{a}$$

If price elasticity and income elasticity are unitary then the relative outlays remain constant:

$$\frac{P_{1t} \cdot X_1}{P_{2t} \cdot X_2} = C$$

However, such a wage-income policy does not change the flow of labour from the progressive to the non-progressive sector.

Another important characteristic of Baumol's production structure is the absence of intermediate demand. In a situation where each of the sectors uses a part of each other's output as inputs, the relative costs will be influenced.

INTERACTION BETWEEN DEMAND AND SUPPLY

The role of demand is not analysed in the unbalanced growth model although the model contains highly relevant implicit demand aspects. An increasing general wage level provides increased income from which increased expenditure for the output of the non-progressive sector can be made [Withers, 1980] and the price changes also cause income-effects. Following Linder [1970] one must recognise that the wage increase through its impact on relative prices and income influences the price of consumption time and forms an incentive to move away from time-intensive consumption activities.

There are a lot of models close to the world of unbalanced growth, which allow for interaction between demand and supply: Simon [1947], Artle, Humes and Varaiya [1977 and 1979], Vislie [1979], Haig [1975], Skolka [1977], Petit [1986] and Worcester [1968].

The discussion of all these models would lead us too far. Smith [1975 and 1978] has incorporated the demand side in the unbalanced growth model in a short but rigorous way and his approach is such that most of the results reported on in the publications cited above are enclosed in his analysis. Therefore we discuss only Smith's general equilibrium framework. Smith translated Baumol's framework into an equilibrium scheme with a production transformation function (supply) and a community utility function (demand):

$$\frac{1}{a} X_{1t} + \frac{1}{b \, e^{rt}} X_{2t} = L_t$$

$$U = (c_1 \, X_{1t}^{-d_1} + c_2 \, X_{2t}^{-d_2})^{-\frac{1}{d}} \qquad \text{(a CRES utility function)}$$

Given these equations Smith proves that:

$$1. \quad \frac{\dot{P_2}}{P_2} - \frac{\dot{P_1}}{P_1} = -r$$

$$2. \quad \frac{\dot{X_1}}{X_{1t}} = \frac{E_I(X_1)}{E_I(X_2)} \cdot \frac{\dot{X_2}}{X_{2t}} - \frac{\sigma}{E_1(X_2)} r$$

The first result shows that relative prices are supply-determined and that the rate of change of relative price is given by the rate of productivity growth in the progressive sector. The last equation provides explicit evidence on the interaction between income elasticities (E_I), the elasticity of substitution (γ) between X_1 and X_2 and the productivity rate (r).

The growth of the non-progressive sector depends on the magnitude of these parameters. The most important implication of all this is:

- that it is not the absolute value of the income elasticity of demand for services that is important but its relative value to the income elasticity of the manufacturing sector.

- that with unitary income elasticities attention has to be given to the extent to which people view X_1 and X_2 as real substitutes.

These conclusions shed some light on the dispute of the emergence of a service economy or a self-service economy [see Gershuny, 1978 and Skolka, 1976].

To test the hypothesis of the development to a self-service economy one has to estimate the magnitude of the elasticity of substitution (γ).

CONCLUSIONS

Taylor's model is very useful if one wishes to simulate how the sectoral structure will develop given the growth of the different components of final demand. But it tells us nothing about the forces causing changes in final demand because demand is supposed to be completely exogeneous. Baumol's model shows that the sectoral composition can influence the overall growth of an economy and from Smith's extension of the unbalanced growth model it becomes clear that the demand and supplyside of an economy are strongly interwoven.

The theoretical models reviewed here reveal these interrelations and show that the change in industrial structure, the growth of each sector and overall growth itself depend on the relative demand and supply characteristics of the different sectors.

The models cannot give a straightforward answer to questions like that of Tinbergen because the concrete effects of demand-push growth policy depend on the numerical value of the demand- and supply parameters. Therefore one can only draw concrete conclusions from carefully designed empirical research. Policies based on rough general rules are dangerous. The weakest points in empirical research in my view with respect to the services industries are:

1. the effects of changes in intermediate demand including the effects of changes in production techniques;
2. international trade of services;
3. structural shift in final demand for services;
4. the substitution phenomenon between goods and services.

In connection with intermediate demand we need a picture of the relations between service industries and the other sectors of the economy. Chenery and Watanabe [1959] developed some interesting measures. Further, we have to calculate intermediate demand growth and try to split up this growth rate in a component which can be explained by the externalisation and internalisation process and a component which is due to real expansion in the demand for intermediate services. De Haan and Tordoir [1986] and Coppietiers [1982, 1986] have undertaken an exploratory research in that field. Within the same context one can analyse if new technologies diminish the labour intensity in the intermediate services.

The approach in the research about trade in services depends too much on balance of trade data. The magnitude of the internal flow of services within multinational firms and groups is an important black hole in our understanding of international trade in services. Close to this topic is the fact that industrial economics neglects the study of characteristics of services markets [Akehurst, 1984, did some work in this field].

This last remark brings us back to the models. If one gets estimations of the evolution of the demand and supply characteristics of service markets (e.g. income- and price-elasticities, productivity changes and substitution elasticities) one can use the models to explain and understand the observed evolution.

REFERENCES

Akehurst, G.P., 1984, 'Checkout: The Analysis of Oligopolistic Behaviour in the UK Grocery Retail Market', *The Service Industries Journal*, Vol. 4, No. 2.

Artle, R., C. Humes and P. Varaiya, 1977, 'Division of Labor-Simon Revisited', *Regional Science and Urban Economics*, Vol. 7, No. 3.

Artle, R., C. Humes and P. Varaiya, 1979, 'Division of Labor and the Distribution of Income', *Regional Science and Urban Economics*, Vol. 9, No. 1.

Baumol, W.J., 1967, 'Macroeconomics of Unbalanced Growth: the Anatomy of Urban Crisis', *The American Economic Review*, Vol. LVII, No. 3.

Bradford, D.F., 1969, 'Balance on Unbalanced Growth', *Zeitschrift für Nationalökonomie*, Vol. 29, No.3.

Chenery, H.B. and T. Watanabe, 1958, 'International Comparisons of the Structure of Production', *Econometrica*, Vol. 26, No. 4.

Chenery, H.B., 1960, 'Patterns of Industrial Growth', *The American Economic Review*, Vol. 50, Sept.

Chenery, H.B., 1960, 'Development Patterns: Among Countries and over Time', *The American Economic Review*, Vol. 58, Nov.

Chenery, H.B. and M. Syrguin, 1975, '*Patterns of Development: 1950-1970*', New York: Oxford University Press.

Clark, G., 1957, *The Conditions of Economic Progress*, London: Macmillan.

Coppieters, P., 1982, '*De Regionale Dimensie van de Tertialisering van de Werkgelegenheid*', Doctoral Dissertion, University of Antwerp, Antwerp.

Coppieters, P., 1986, *Het Belang van de Tertiaire Sector voor de Vlaamse Economie*, Brussels: Adviesraad D.I.R.V.

de Hann, M.A. and P.P. Tordoir, 1986, *Belang van Diensten voor de Nederlandse Economie*, Delft: Planologisch Studiecentrum TNO.

Fisher, A.G.B., 1983, 'Capital and the Growth of Knowledge', *The Economic Journal*, Vol. 63, No. 171.

Fourastié, J., 1949, *Le Grand espoir du XXe siècle*, Paris: P.U.F.

Gershuny, J.I., 1978, *After Industrial Society?*, London: Macmillan.

Haig, D.B., 1975, 'An Analysis of Changes in the Distribution of Employment between the Manufacturing and Service Industries 1960-1970', *The Review of Economics and Statistics*.

Linder, S.B., 1970, *The Harried Leisure Class*, Columbia University Press, New York.

Nonneman, W. and M. De Wachter, 1976, 'The Allocation of Labour and Wage-Income Policies', SESO-Werknota 7665, University of Antwerp, Antwerp.

Petit, P., 1986, *Slow Growth and the Service Economy*, London: Frances Pinter.

Simon, H.A., 1947, 'Effects of Increased Productivity upon the Ratio of Urban to Rural Population', *Econometrica*, Vol. 15, No. 1.

Skolka, J.V., 1976, 'The Substitution of Self-service Activities for Marketed Services', *The*

Review of Income and Wealth, Vol. 22, No. 4.

Skolka, J.V., 1977, 'Unbalanced Productivity Growth and the Growth of Public Services', *Journal of Public Economics*, Vol. 7, No. 2.

Smith, V.K., 1975, 'A Note on Baumol's Unbalanced Growth Model', *Public Finance*, Vol. 30, No. 1.

Smith, V.K., 1978, 'Unbalanced Productivity Growth and the Growth of Public Services', *Journal of Public Economics*, Vol. 10, No. 1.

Taylor, L.J., 1969, 'Development Patterns: A Simulation Study', *Quarterly Journal of Economics*, Vol. 83, No.2.

Tinbergen, J., 1980, 'Which Sectors Should be Stimulated by a Recovery Policy?', *Lloyds Bank Review*, No.137.

Vislie, J., 1979, 'Division of Labor–Simon Revisited. A Comment', *Regional Science and Urban Economics*, Vol. 9, No.1.

Withers, G.A., 1980, 'Unbalanced Growth and the Demand for Performing Arts', *Southern Economic Journal*, Vol. 46, No. 3.

Worcester, D.A., 1968, 'Macroeconomics of Unbalanced Growth: Comment', *American Economic Review*, Vol. 58, No. 4.

The New Deal in Services – A Challenge for Europe

by

Olivier Ruyssen*

This article is based upon surveys on services and their development carried out by 15 European research centres, within the context of the FAST programme of the European Communities' Committee.

After an analysis of why the question of services is the object of growing attention on the part of governments, some of the aspects analysed by FAST, such as the new technology/service interaction and the change in the productive system are considered, and the implications of these evolutions for the community policies are discussed.

WHY SERVICES?

The service economy has been the object of a renewed interest in recent years for at least three reasons. First, the service sector has supplied a *great number of jobs* whereas industrial employment is declining or stagnating. This fact, particularly strong in the United States, drew attention at a time when growing unemployment was becoming a major issue in most countries (Table 1).

TABLE 1

SERVICE SECTOR JOBS AND UNEMPLOYMENT

	Jobs in services (number in thousands)			Unemployment (in thousands)		
	1979	1984		1979	1984	
Eur. 10	56,619	61,119	+4,500	5,686	12,430	+6,744
Germany	12,240	13,025	+ 785	851	2,265	+1,414
France	11,584	12,371	+ 787	1,266	2,309	+1,043
Italy	14,433	15,237	+ 804	1,310	3,160	+1,850
United K	9,929	10,954	+1,325	1,521	2,719	+1,198
USA	63,088	71,644	+8,556	5,623	7,770	+2,147

Source: Eurostat

*The author is expressing personal views in this paper.

The first question asked of Europeans is the following: Is growth through services likely and could it represent an answer to unemployment? The answer seems to be 'yes' in the United States, where, as an alternative to unemployment, unskilled, more or less precarious or atypical service jobs are accepted. A high percentage of the new service jobs actually show these characteristics (cleaning staff, nursing auxiliaries, salesmen, cashiers, bartenders, janitors, clerks) and are part-time or temporary jobs. And nearly 90 per cent of the 20 million new jobs created in the USA in the last ten years were service jobs.

Such a pattern is not easy to judge. It can be seen as a way of sharing employment and of keeping the largest number of people employed even if it means they do have interruptions. Or it can also be seen as a 'dualisation' of American society, between those who have a 'real job' and those who are restricted to petty jobs. If the transposition of this pattern to Europe seems difficult for economic, cultural and social reasons, measures can certainly be taken to facilitate the birth and development of numerous tertiary activities often penalised by too rigid legislations.

The second cause comes from the fact that, for a number of countries (except Japan, Canada and Germany) the service sector is *a net source of currency* while goods exchanges are in deficit.

TABLE 2

THE SERVICE SECTOR AS A SOURCE OF CURRENCY

BALANCE OF GOODS and SERVICES (1984) –millions of ECU–

	Goods	Services
Germany	27,635	– 5,540
France	– 5,043	+ 8,852
Italy	– 7,805	+ 2,642
United Kingdom	– 7,194	+12,337
USA	–137,739	+23,667

It is this observation which led the United States to set the cat among the pigeons in November 1982 at the GATT. As they noticed their precious surplus in services getting smaller year after year and they thought that this reduction was coming from a growing protectionism on the part of their customers and competitors, the USA vigorously demanded that the international community should tackle the non-tariff barriers of the exchange of services. Launching a series of national surveys on services within the context of the GATT research studies, has been an important factor of stimulation to analyse the role of services.

In this context, the question which is asked of the European Community is not so much whether its economic benefit (but also its political advantage) is in adjusting the existing status quo (one sector after another, with bilateral agreements) or in setting up a general policy with a view to liberalising exchanges, but rather whether the European firms that are able to export services see any possibility of being competitive on world markets. We must stress straightaway that we lack data on this matter.

The fact that the Community is a net exporter of services is certainly a positive factor of estimation, but it must not be the only one. We must know whether Europe is in a good position in the competition for developing markets (high-level services to firms for example, such as consultancy or financial engineering) and whether European firms will be able to control the significant components of services competition in the long term. We will study this question again when we come to the 'meta-industrialisation' challenge.

For the Community, liberalising exchanges also means adapting its own market. For that matter, a precise schedule has been decided on, with the goal of achieving a big European 'border-free' market for 1992. The goal is difficult to reach in the case of services, for many professions are controlled differently from one country to another. Moreover, a great number of services and technological products, being closely linked, means the free flow of services is hindered by problems of technical compatibility between equipment produced according to different norms and standards in the different countries.

The third reason is related to the current *technological changes* occurring around the unquestionable boom of the new technologies in information and communication. This new technological 'deal' is at the heart of the transformation of our economies and of our societies, and is strongly affecting both the nature of a number of services and their strategic meaning in the development process. The studies carried out within the context of the FAST programme (especially SEMA, 1986; CURDS, 1986; CEPS, 1986; GARNIER, 1986) have tried to clarify the directions and scope of this transformation.

NEW TECHNOLOGIES AND SERVICES: A DIFFICULT INTEGRATION

The new technologies have a double impact on service activities. First, implementing them in the production process requires information, training, installation and maintenance services. Then, the final user must be helped in his choice and use of more and more complex products. Therefore, when you resort to new technologies you need services to produce and services to sell at your permanent disposal.

The New Technologies of Communication and Information (NTCI) are mostly those that considerably change the way in which most services are supplied, since, very often a service consists in transforming information and distributing it. In fact, some authors, drawing their inspiration from Porat's research studies, consider that, on the whole, all the people whose jobs are in services spend from 45 to 80 per cent of their time on transforming information and distributing it (education and training, legal services, media, travel agencies, consultancy, management, different civil services, security, medical services . . .) The communication process often demands a *direct contact* (face-to-face) between the service provider and his customer, at one time or another.

More generally, the relations between 'provider' and 'consumer' are often much closer in the case of services than in the case of material goods. One only has to think of the work of teachers and trainers, of consultants, of doctors, of most liberal professions. Hence, the importance of the 'customisation' process (this is what Toffler calls 'prosumerism' [Toffler, 1970]) and of the necessary proximity between service providers and consumers.

The coupling of NTCI and services, especially at company levels finds expression first and foremost in the rapid growth of some activities, as shown in Table 3: the jobs supplied by data processing and office automation are among the leading occupations ranked according to the expected rate of growth between 1984 and 1995 (Table 3).

TABLE 3

FASTEST GROWING OCCUPATIONS, 1984-95

OCCUPATION	Employment		Change in employment 1984-95		Percent of total job growth
	1984	1985	Number	Percent	1984-95
Paralegal personnel	53	104	51	97,5	3
Computer programmers	341	586	245	71,7	1,5
Computer systems analysts	308	520	212	68,7	1,3
Medical assistants	128	207	79	62,0	5
Data processing equipment repairers	50	78	28	56,2	2
Electrical and electronics engineers	390	597	206	52,8	1,3
Electrical and electronics technicians	404	607	202	50,7	1,3
Computer operators	241	353	111	46,1	7
Peripheral EDP equipment operators	70	102	32	45,0	2
Travel agents	72	103	32	43,9	2

Source: Monthly Labor Review, Nov. 1985.

New technology also finds expression in the fact that a number of services are becoming more easily transported, accessible day and night and from anywhere on the globe. And lastly, it also finds expression in increased possibilities of substitutions between goods and services or services supplied under a new form (self-service).

For a longer-term forecast, three questions can be asked:

- are we heading for a high standardisation of services thanks to our mastering of the automated processing information?
- are we heading for an increase in the number of 'tele-services' coming from a likely slackening of the proximity constraint thanks to the improvements in NTCI?
- are we going to witness the blossoming of a series of 'new services' associated with the improvements in the NTCI, and will there be an important growth of corresponding jobs?

Today, it seems that in each case the answer must be quantified. NTCI are mostly used in services to allow productivity increases and they find their expression in a *standardisation* of the service: in order to automate the production and distribution of the service as much as possible, it is codified and normalised. Economies of scale becoming possible, production can be concentrated and the market internationalised.

But the standardisation of the service goes with a necessary simplification (and sometimes over-simplification) of its contents. Then we can see a new market segmentation emerge, with, on the one hand, a minimum service supplied to a large group of customers and on the other hand *customised* services added to the minimum service or independent from them and better adapted to the specific needs of some groups of users. As to production strategies, we can witness the development of two separate industries (it is often the case for software for instance, with the industry of standard software often supplied with the equipment and that of customised software, of highly-added value because of a high investment in human resources) or the development of industries that sell complex and flexible 'packages' associating standardised *and* customised services on demand, as in the case of financial services of information brokers (for instance).

The future trend seems to be the development of the 'package' strategy which will maintain the necessity of contacts with the user and will simultaneously bring about a quantitative and qualitative development of telecommunication networks. We must then seek to know whether through a relaxing of the *proximity constraint* between the service provider and his customer, NTCI will bring about a fundamental change in the dynamics of the location of service activities. In theory the answer is yes.

Different techniques enable us to communicate, to process information and to work at a distance, at a tolerable financial cost. Observers think that the decentralisation of production units will continue, without, however, reaching the point of replacement of large units, for economies of scale remain a fact and there are limits to the flexibility of automated units.

The decentralisation of different administrative tasks is common to large groups. There are potentialities in telework, teleshopping and telebanking. Some systems (videotex, teletext) enable households and firms to have direct access to a number of services and the service networks (e.g. VANS, ISDN) are booming, though their development is quite unequal from one area to the other. However,the experience we have now of teleservices shows that, most of the time, it is a matter of complementarity but not of substitution, between the 'new' teleservice and the traditional face-to-face service. For example, telework will probably develop but all the studies on the subject insist that the 'teleworker' will have to visit the firm frequently, which will maintain the proximity constraint.

As for the 'new services', they are often former activities which have been more or less transformed because of our resorting to new technologies. As they become more effective and further-reaching the demand for them grows and they become subject to rapid expansion. This pattern, mentioned earlier, is first and foremost a fact in companies and is concentrated on the services of access to information and the jobs that go with them. It is and will remain much more limited in the sphere of services to private individuals, for reasons which are mainly financial because of the high costs of both services and the necessary equipment for their production/consumption, or because of the lack of the necessary skills to implement them, but above all, because of an imperfect match between services supplied and private individuals' needs. A good example is the Minitel and videotex services in France. At the beginning of 1986, more than 1.5 million terminals were installed in firms or households and approximately 3000 different services were supplied to the users. The jobs created around these 'new services' did not exceed 8000. Results seem to be similar in other countries developing telematics services (United Kingdom, the Netherlands, Germany).

As a temporary conclusion, we can say that the integration between new technologies and services is following rather different developments, but no simple pattern seems to be prominent. The speed at which it is being achieved is also quite different according to the different spheres, therefore introducing distinctions between those who have access to and profit from the 'new services', and the rest. Reducing the existing gaps between individuals, socio-professional groups, companies and regions is a major challenge. We will examine what it is like at the European Community level.

THE 'META-INDUSTRIALISATION' CHALLENGE

Some research scholars see in services-to-company dynamics a sign of considerable change in the production system. The services supplied to firms represent more than one third of the marketed services. They include financial services, information services, research/development, legal services, public relations, management, administrative services, etc. . . They constitute the medium of the 'meta-industrialisation'.

Research scholars call this process 'meta-industrialisation' [Olivry, 1986], meaning that this change does not lead to a 'post-industrial' society, over-tertiarised and concentrated on services to people, but rather that industrial activity remains central while changing shapes.

The development of service activities is therefore not an independent process but is achieved in a permanent interaction with the meta-industrialisation process on an international level as on an internal level or company level. We can describe this evolution from the industrial stage to the 'meta-industrial' stage as:

- markets being more and more on a world scale *and* segmented;
- 'products' consisting of goods *and* services, with really low added value standardised elements and high added value customised elements adapted to the users' specific needs;
- more and more flexible production systems, able to change from large mass-production to small-scale production with a very high proportion of information technologies (the 'intelligent' workshop);

- the development of a new technical, managerial, organisational culture;
- the development of internal oligopolies *and* that of small companies having an efficient 'niche' or gap strategy;
- increased competition *and* a simultaneous co-operation and partnership development (technical, marketing, financial);
- an increased number of skilled and highly-skilled workers at both 'blue collar' and 'white collar' levels.
- a cellular productive network organisation often linking very different company structures (very large firms *and* small firms);
- complex sectorial structures with trans-sectorial differentiated and hyper-specialised companies;
- very close contact between company and customers;
- less rigid social relations within the company, increased relations with institutions;
- increased resort to services (buying *and* selling specialised services) finding its expression in new internationalised and externalised strategies of services.

For the next 20 years, this meta-industrialisation process seems to be irreversible for it is situated in the present technological, economic and social evolution. It seems necessary, for it is the condition of both company efficiency and company competitivity, and of a more adaptable and flexible link between economic necessities and social longings. Lastly, it seems useful because it intensifies the dynamics of the entrepreneurial and regional development which a number of the EEC regions lack. A 'meta-industrialisation' policy is therefore necessary at the Community level. We must analyse its components.

THE IMPLICATIONS FOR COMMON POLICIES

The common policies developed today have many links, not surprisingly, with the services and meta-industrialisation. We must check if the general directions agreed or contribute to creating a service-friendly environment and if they allow us to make the best of the meta-industrialisation process. Without going into details, two priorities seem to stand out when we examine things from a Community angle.

The first is about guaranteed *access to services*. In fact, *at the level of each company* (large or small-owned or privately held, central or regional) the meta-industrialisation challenge requires a necessary access to NTCI, that is to say to facilities (machines, networks, infrastructures) and *above all to the expert competence necessary for their implementation*. It also requires a necessary access to a whole range of services (information, legal, financial) at the lowest cost.

The Community must provide this guarantee by ensuring a competition as free as possible. Hence the importance of the efforts made to achieve a *market free of borders* and to develop international negotiations on liberalising service exchanges.

But removing barriers is not sufficient. In fact, trends for the next 20 years are the simultaneous concentration of skills, of specialised services for equipment and of infrastructures in some regions and in some big industrial concerns. (The mechanisms of such a concentration are analysed in various FAST papers and summed up in the FAST Strategic File 'Service and Region Development' DOS 4.). This concentration intensifies the efficiency and competitiveness of the companies that know how to profit from it.

It also represents *a real obstacle for the long-term economic integration of the Community* by widening the disparities between the different regions and different companies, and leaving the least favoured ones irreversibly out of the modernisation and transformation process which is worldwide. Overcoming this obstacle has become a must for the EEC common policies. We must therefore strengthen our structures to enable most companies and households to have access to the meta-industrialisation components (access to NTCI, to knowledge, to expert evaluation) and thereby increase the efficiency, reliability and cohesion of the European productive system. If we rely on the structures which have often already been implemented in member-states it implies:

- developing the *infrastructures* for meta-industrialisation (tele-communication networks but also training centres, technological exchanges, local supply of services to companies) in under-developed regions first. In fact the regional tolerance for 'man-made' comparative significant advantage endowment happens to be wider when seen from the meta-industrialisation angle, as is shown in Table 4.
- giving a bigger help for access to specialised services, to innovations, to markets, within the programmes aimed at the *small and medium-sized companies;*
- orienting differently the Science and Technology policies (espec-ially within the new context of the 'Unique Act') by establishing a better balance between the programmes aimed at developing technology supply and the steps aimed at making sure it is *distributed and used.*
- the second priority is related to intensifying European capabilites regards *the supply of strategic services.* In this respect, the first thing seems to be to acquire a *sound understanding of the situation* in the competition of the different supply 'sectors'. We have already mentioned that we lack this understanding. Acquiring this understanding is urgent in order to determine where our strong and weak points lie. Adapting our policies accordingly is urgent too, especially at international summits.

It implies that we should acquire the necessary tools, and an operational statistics base. Observatories, research programmes or centres working on different sectors (legal services, information services for example) will have to be created or intensified. It also implies that we should have an *educational and training system* adapted to the needs of meta-industrial societies. The 'meta-industrial' organisations will need to master man–machine and man-to-man communications even better than today. They will have to make complex human structures work efficiently, then they will have to perfect and use all sorts of information communications systems.

At the same time, interpersonal relations within firms, firm-to-firm, provider-to-customer are becoming more and more important. There again, the growth of the service activities which are often characterised by intense man-to-man relations is revealing. Therefore, next to the engineer who is there to carry through the material processing successfully and to ensure the smooth running of the machines, have successively appeared the marketing specialist, the financier, the management consultant, the public relations officer, the social relations specialist. The 'meta-industrial' man will have to be a mixture of each of these. And it is at this very level that the major challenge of years to come is situated.

Our educational and professional training systems may not be up to it. Their adjustment will require a considerable effort which is really out of the reach of the Community's traditional means of action. This education and training challenge gets even more complicated because, to be developed efficiently, the 'new jobs' mentioned earlier will have to rely on a new scientific corpus. The scientific mastery of such a corpus is a basic challenge in the long term.

Next, after the necessary progress in the sciences of the materials, we must have the basic components for the development of communication and advanced information networks (optical fibres, chips, receivers, transmitters). Some leads are opening ahead to *intensify the Community foundations* not only in cognitive sciences, in advanced languages, in algorithmics, but also in behaviourial and communication sciences, etc. Research studies in these fields exist in the community. But the effort seems insufficient. The co-ordination of the different studies is essential. A common programme is then necessary and unified work should be undertaken.

Besides these two priorities, and also on a long-term prospect, we will, in all likelihood, have to tackle some aspects of the economic and social system regulation. In fact, a statutory framework has been set up to run an economic system centred on goods to run an industrial economy.

The change to a meta-industrial economy in which immaterial activities are playing a key-role leads us to question the judiciousness of such a framework. For example:

- the accounting and tax reliefs for investment should be reconsidered when it concerns an intangible investment (investment in research and development, in trade or marketing, in training, . . .)
- the rules and regulations on work are not always well-adapted to the characteristics of service activities (adaptable working-times,

work done at home or away from the plant, atypical jobs);
- in other instances, the determining criteria to get state support are to be re-examined to allow tertiary companies to receive support like other classical manufacturing companies.

Beyond these few examples, we come to wonder if,when a nation's wealth is stemming from these so-called unproductive activities, it is not the economy as a whole that we should re-think.

ORGANISING A DIALOGUE

Although cautiously leaving this task to others, we should only say that, through these different aspects, some action is necessary. Faced with the uncertainties of meta-industrialisation, a huge clarifying and pioneering work remains to be done. All the actors of meta-industrialisation (large and small companies) are concerned. Prompting meeting and dialogue opportunities within the Community, suggesting debates, rallying executives, structuring research work, organising seminars – these are the short-term tasks to achieve.

TABLE 4

COMPONENTS AND SOURCES OF THE COMPARATIVE ADVANTAGE IN SERVICES

a. COMPARATIVE SIGNIFICANT ADVANTAGES

MANUFACTURING INDUSTRIES (Production of goods)	META-INDUSTRIES (Production of goods and services)
• Access to raw materials	• Access to information, to expert evaluation
• Wages	• Wages
• Meek Labour/'Blue Collars'	• Skilled Labour/'Gold Collars'
• Goods exchange systems	• Functional relational systems
• Goods transport networks	• Telecommunication and people transport networks.

TABLE 4 (continued)

b. ADVANTAGE SOURCES – INPUT ENDOWMENT

Natural	*Created out of Region*	*Created within Region*
• Geology, climate	(*) Infrastructures	(*) Infrastructures
• Geographical location	(*) Regulation	(*) Data bases
• Size and proximity of markets	• Tax system	(**) Training centres
	• Political alliances	• Structures of labour market
• Population	• State sector/ Private sector relations	• Wage levels Risk capital
	• Financial system	(*) Partnership networks (commercial and industrial
	• Purchasing power	alliances, firms/schools relations).
		• Local authorities/ private sector relations
		(*) Intermediation services Cultural services Local social relationships Image, skill assertion

(*) = key-factors for 'meta-industries'.

Sources: FAST (From D. Riddle, 1986, and SEMA, 1986).

REFERENCES

Barras, R., *et al.,* 1986, 'Technical Tools fo the new Services', FAST occasional paper no. 68, London: Technical Change Centre.

Bressand, A., *et al.,* 1986, 'Europe and the New International Division of Labor in the Field of Services', FAST occasional papers Nos. 127 and 128, PROMETHEE-CEPII-CEPS.

Garnier, G., 1986, 'Worldwide and Local Technologies', a FAST exploratory dossier, CEE.

Howell, J., 1987, 'Trends in the Location, Technological Innovation and Industrial Organisation of Services in the European Community. Regional Economic Development Prospects', FAST occasional paper No.142, CURDS.

Olivry, D., 1986, 'Services to the Manufacturing Sector – A Long Term Investigation', FAST occasional papers Nos.96 and 97, SEMA.

Riddle, D., 1986, *Service-led Growth*, New York: Praeger.

Ruyssen, O., 1987, 'Nouvelles Technologies, Services et Régions', a FAST strategic dossier, CEE.

Toffler, A., 1970, *Future Shock*, New York: Random House.

From the Rigidity of Supply to the Service Economy

by

Orio Giarini and Jean Rémy Roulet

A series of hypotheses are put forward in an effort to understand the origin and development of production activities which are services. In addition it is necessary to understand why economic theory has failed to consider services as a motor for growth. Service industries appear to be the main way to reduce the rigidities of economic structure and manage risks and uncertainties.

INTRODUCTION

According to J.S. Mill [1871: 46], work serves to 'produce three types of utilities: utility embodied in external material things, utility embodied in human beings (like education), and utility not fixed or embodied in any object'.

Today hardly anyone would disagree with the English economist on this point. If, however, he were to go on to say that only the first type of work is productive (as A. Smith [1776] said before him) he would be contradicting the fact that 70 per cent of the work-force of our Western economies is involved in reputedly non-productive activities – services [Riddle, 1986].

It must, however, be admitted that he cannot be considered as voluntarily being wrong. His days were marked by the repercussions of the industrial revolution, the growth in wealth and welfare of a nation accompanied by a quantitative increase in consumer goods. Indeed, it is this unequivocal relationship which constitutes the foundations of classical economic theory, as it is still taught today. Do not a firm's profits come from a maximisation of the product price by the quantity of goods to produce? Is not the welfare of a consumer measured by the maximisation of a utility function, the main arguments of which are the price and the quantity of goods he consumes?

The aims of this essay are twofold: on the one hand it puts forward a series of hypotheses which would make it easier to understand the origin of the development of these (henceforth) production activities which are services. On the other hand it is necessary to understand why economic theory omitted to take into consideration the vital importance of service activities as a motor for growth, and supply some elements of a solution for a re-conceptualisation of certain premises specific to this theory. It seems right today to inquire whether classic programmes of maximisation resulting from the industrial revolution era can give a valid explanation of the economic world which surrounds us. Straightaway we would like to give the reader what we consider as the lesson to be learnt from this exercise: to speak of a service economy means making a tentative appraisal of contemporary economy as it is, and also identifying the means of stimulating its development. It is in this way that the service economy is defined as an economy in which the functions of service have become production inputs, henceforth mobilising the relatively largest part of resources. In other words, these activities represent the greatest cost to produce economic wealth in the world today.

THE SERVICE ECONOMY

The growth of service functions in the production of wealth

The growth of service functions is a direct result of the development of production techniques which have succeeded each other since the Industrial Revolution. Up to the beginning of the twentieth century, the improvement of new technologies and the changes in production methods came, for the most part, from the accumulated experience of man at his machine. Such changes and improvements were only very rarely the result of organised work and financed by a research centre.

The professionalisation of research began round about the 1920s reflecting the growing complexity of new technologies and the need to scrupulously plan and develop their creation. This service function 'research' today occupies millions of people and attracts a considerable share of budgets from both the private and public sectors.

The service functions 'maintenance' (upkeep) and 'storage' of input and output could formerly be considered as integrated parts of the production system, in a simple industrialisation phase. However, the growing specialisation of production units (input) as well as the more and more complex technology applied in these production units have created a more than proportional development of these service functions. One of the main economic consequences of this growing complexity of the whole production machine has been the relative drop in the cost of pure production compared with the costs created by service functions.[1]

Today a product can no longer be accessible to the consumer without going through complex operations of promotion and organisation of the market, among other things ensuring the distribution of any product to more and more varied geographical destinations, to increasing numbers of consumers or to greater distances from the place of production. The more 'advanced' the 'product', the more must be invested in order to learn how to use it.

Financial activity as well as the service function 'insurance' linked to the performance of the product and its distribution have also become indispensable. This statement would appear trivial to the builders of nuclear power stations or oil rigs which call for investment commonly going beyond a billion dollars. The more our society tends towards a complex production system, the more the laws governing the various agents will become adapted. Agents in their turn will become more specialised, and will come up against problems of vulnerablilty. Other service functions, such as health and national defence, are becoming also increasingly important in our contemporary economies. It is essential to consider the growth of service functions (as the result of the specific evolution of the production system) to understand and correctly evaluate modern society. The development of the technology which increased the efficiency of the production process, leads to the development of service functions at every level of transformation and utilisation of that input.

All the above mentioned service functions are to be found essentially in planification, from production to the moment of sale and even beyond the exchange, during the utilisation period of the product. However, the maturing of the economy following the Industrial Revolution has brought out another indispensable service function: waste management. Waste has always been a side product from any type of activity and from human production e.g., peeling a banana creates waste. When the Industrial Revolution brought a great movement towards concentration and production specialisation, inevitably waste began to concentrate and accumulate in turn. This is not necessarily a negative phenomenon. Throughout the history of the Industrial Revolution, waste was often turned into side products and even into new main products. To give a few examples, base fertilisers originated in the explosives industry, and phosporus used as a detergent or fertiliser came from the iron and steel industry's waste. However, an increasingly awkward problem arose in the field of the most advanced technologies – how can waste, which is non-profitable and which cannot be transformed into utilisable products, be managed? Generally speaking, this phenomenon can be observed each time the principle of the specialisation of products reaches its operational limits. Furthermore a large quantity of new products derived from the latest manipulations in physics and chemistry has increased the complexity of waste. This has also led to an increase in the frequency and intensity of the risk created by such manipulations. The concentration, specialisation and increased level of dangerous side effects are henceforth the negative result of the use of more sophisticated multi-sector technology, and are based on the latest scientific progress. More and more resources must be given over to controlling this phenomenon. Alongside this growth in industrial waste, the obvious increase in individual consumption cannot be forgotten. This consumption has increased the quantity of waste produced by millions of consumers, both in terms of quality and quantity: a plastic bottle cannot always be burned in the same way as a piece of wood or paper. It can give off corroding and even toxic fumes. Considerable investment therefore is needed in order to organise an efficient and appropriate waste disposal system. All products, all matter (including our own bodies) become waste. It is possible to transform some of this waste, after its cycle of production and utilisation, into new raw material. This transformation process occurs quite naturally in certain cases, for example organic matter, Sometimes it requires a certain length of time including the recycling activity carried out by man. Two limits are reached in the recycling of waste economic entropy (prohibitive cost of recycling) and physical entropy (when the recycling cannot be carried out for physical reasons).[2] The handling, destruction and recycling of waste as from that moment became a crucial subject in the service economy.

A typical work hypothesis of the Industrial Revolution era consists in considering the production process as finished the moment the product becomes available on the market. In the service economy, the complete act of production finishes when the utilisation of the products and services have been maximised throughout their life period and when the following are taken into account:

- pre-production costs,
- production costs,
- post-production costs.

The growth in industrialisation of service activities

The development of the service economy which can be seen all around us should be considered as a global process arising from the Industrial Revolution rather than as simply the result of a passing growth to be seen in certain traditional service activities. After all, service functions are integrated in all production activities, from the agricultural sector to industrial sectors. It is also essential to understand that modern technology has radically changed the method of work for a large part of traditional services. This change has also brought about a high increase in the need for the factor capital in the services production processes, which is very similar to what could be seen at the outset of the Industrial Revolution. The difference between computerising functions as carried out in an office and the 'intelligent' production control centre in a firm are rapidly disappearing.

This led certain authors to speak of contemporary economy as being a 'super-industrial' or a 'Third Industrial Revolution' type economy instead of referring to it as a service economy [Leveson, 1985]. In considering the sectors of leading industries, these authors point to the fact that traditional service activities are undergoing an industrialisation process. It is obvious that this phenomenon is still important, but it does not take into account the spectacular increase in service functions within the traditional sectors of production. It would be wrong to believe that the development of telecommunications, banking, financial and insurance services, maintenance and engineering services are all simply the expression of a new form of production similar to what happened in the textile, iron and steel or chemical industries.

The horizontal integration of all production activities: an end to the theory of the three sectors and the limits to Engel's Law

Traditional economic theory still distinguishes three sectors of production activities: the primary or agricultural, the secondary or industrial and the tertiary sector including all the services [Fourastié, 1958]. This vertical division into sectors has led to theories on economic development according to which there is a historical transition from agricultural to industrial societies and in the present time from industrial to service societies. This kind of theory is mainly based on the industrialisation process where predominantly agricultural societies are those which are not yet industrial and where the tertiary sector more often than not serves as a 'trash can' in which is placed all economic activity which cannot simply be called 'industrial activity' [Shelp, 1981].

In fact for these three types of society, (agricultural, industrial or service), it become crucially important to establish the priorities which make it possible to stimulate and improve the production of wealth and welfare.

In an industrial society, however, agriculture does not disappear; indeed on the contrary its production becomes more efficient, thanks to the industrialisation process which fits into the traditional chain of production and distribution of farm produce. In the same way the service economy is not a cyclical outgrowth coming from the structure of industrial production [Gershuny and Miles, 1983]. It also fits into this structure and becomes indispensable to the working of the whole production system. To sum up, the real phenomenon which can be observed is the progressive horizontal interpenetration of the three sectors and not the decline or growth of any particular one of them. In other words the new service economy does not correspond to the tertiary sector in the traditional way, but is based on the fact that service functions dominate all other types of economic activity. If this statement is accepted then other notions such as that of essential needs take on other meanings.

In an agricultural society, any production system has been designed to satisfy essential (primary) needs; this is obvious. Ever since the Industrial Revolution era every need has been defined as an essential need satisfied by the manufacturing system of production. At least this is what has been maintained by the classical economic theory which up to now has been inspired by the evolution of the industrialisation process. Engel's law states that services only satisfy secondary needs (subordinate to primary needs) in most cases. In this light, the Industrial Revolution is supposed to represent an efficient method for supplying food, shelter and health to people. It is only when these needs are satisfied that certain services can be consumed. However, the real change resulting from the service society comes from the fact that it is precisely these services which have become indispensable for traditional goods and services to satisfy primary needs. In a service economy goods are only *utilisable* thanks to the functioning of these services.

The insurance field is a typical example. Up to the 1970s everyone (including insurance people) described insurance as a secondary activity in the traditional economic meaning: this market could only expand once the primary needs were satisfied. However, during the years that followed the 1973 crisis, world production slumped by 3 per cent per year, whereas the total sale of insurance policies on a worldwide level continued to increase by 5 per cent per year. If insurance consumption had been of secondary importance, the slowing down of activities producing primary goods would have created a proportional drop in the sale of policies, according to Engel's law.

Such a growth in a background of relative crisis mainly reflects the fact that the modern production system is today based on service functions of the insurance type. In the same way on a more national scale, social security, health and life insurance have acquired the status of primary needs in most industrialised countries nowadays.

From the value of a product to the value of a system

Considering the notion of value, there is another fundamental distinction separating the industrial from the service economy. The first gives a value to all exchangeable products, whereas the latter attributes value to the performance and real utilisation (for a given period of time) of products integrated in a system. Whereas in a classical industrial economy, the value of a product equals the sum of the costs entailed in its the production, the notion of value in a service economy equals the amounts put in to obtain results in the utilisation of the same product. In this way it is possible to appreciate more fully the value of non-monetary values.

To sell a product at a given moment in time is a different activity from that which consists in signing a contract of maintenance for a given period of time during which the seller remains linked by contract with the consumer who is using the same product. The essential point to be understood here is that selling in a traditional sense of the term no longer means the same thing in a service economy. In the second meaning, the sale no longer covers only the traditional input when calculating the cost, but also the maintenance costs together with possible costs of replacement. This product is therefore appreciated at its utilisation value.

To what extent the two approaches can be applied depends on the technological complexity in the product. In the case of simple tools the evaluation of the value can be limited to the tool itself. No-one buying a hammer would dream of taking lessons on how to use the tool. However, in the case of a computer, the cost of learning is often greater than that of the machine's purchase price, especially if the cost of buying the software is added.

Whereas in an industrial economy, the question was : 'What is the price-based value of a product?', the service economy asks other questions:

- What is the utilisation value of the product?

- Does it work well and for how long? [Barcet and Bonamy, 1986, p.12]

In a service economy what is bought is the functioning of an object or a system, and no longer the object itself.

The same type of concept can be applied to the health sector. For reasons that are clearly linked to the development of the service economy, institutions called 'Health Maintenance Organisations' (HMO) are developing more and more in the United States. These organisations bring together several elements: guidelines indicating to doctors the need to produce patients who are healthy rather then being heavy consumers of medicine and hospital services; a collaboration between general and specialised doctors, between doctors and chemists; the use of new technologies to record all the useful data concerning a patient's medical history; a drop in public health spending. The success in America of the HMOs has made it possible for patients to receive better treatment and reduced costs in the health sector, because the aim is to optimise a system and not exclusively a sum of money. The money has been spent in a more efficient way because first of all the aim is the performance and the results (improved health) of a system rather than the performance and results of a small sub-system (establish, for example, a correlation between an increase in medicine and an improvement in health) [Gadrey, 1986].

If more and more systematically the accent is put on measuring the results of the functioning of a system, then qualitative and non-monetary considerations will in turn become more pertinent. In some hospitals, the patients are taught to participate more actively in their health care not only to relieve their own suffering but also to bring down the overhead costs of nursing care.

These 'self-service' administration systems contain an intelligent mixture of monetary and non-monetary activities. HMOs are sometimes criticised because they are unusable by part of the population in a worse state of health (the selection effect). It is at this point that social programmes have a positive complementary role to play.

In this way it is necessary to realise that an evaluation of the performance of a system and its results also makes it easy to identify the percentage of non-monetarised activities inherent in the system. To sum up, the notion of utilisation value only has any meaning if, in any economic calculation, account is taken of the life expectancy of products available on the market. This availability is obtained in the function of supply and this supply in turn calls for some specific attention.

SUPPLY AND ECONOMIC THEORY

Supply in the classical economic theory

The economist, like the man in the street, admits that the world is still dominated by a situation of scarcity (material or immaterial) and this in spite of an abundance of natural resources and the wealth of human culture. Working from this statement, J.B. Say proposes the following: in a world or scarcity, all production will be consumed one day or another. the driving force of the economy is therefore, according to him, supply.

The classical economists, from Adam Smith to Ricardo and even to Marx, were 'economists of supply'. One of the key concepts of contemporary economics they have elaborated is that of value. In their view, value is closely linked to the notion of production. As regards price, this is used as a quantitative reference for the value of the product to be sold. The money collected by this sale is used to pay off the factors of production (in the form of salary for the work done by the work-force and in the form of interest for the capital).

In this way all the classical economists, looking for the best way of developing the wealth of nations, whatever their political aspirations might have been, were essentially 'economists of supply'. This was perfectly in keeping with the reality of their times. However, what the old economic theoreticians missed out was the link between the process of monetaris-ation of the economy and industrialisation. This link means Say's Law (because there is scarcity there will sooner or later be distribution of all production) no longer holds true. In the pre-industrial (or agricultural) society, where monetary flow was practically non-existent, all production was consumed immediately. The growth of the monetary systems in our economies therefore went hand in hand with their industrialisation, which meant that production, exchange and consumption of goods and services was more and more dependent on the quantity of available money on the market. Thus a monetary crisis became possible and with it an economic crisis.

The other phenomenon which was underestimated at that time was the development of technology. Science was considered essentially in its cultural and ideological forms. It was only during the first decades of this century that the power of new technologies was realised: the considerable potential growth in production. These two phenomena, the process of monetarisation on the one hand, and the development of technology on the other hand, make up the two explaining factors which are often underestimated in most economic crises in the history of economics.

This movement of great industrial expansion on the beginning of the century accelerated in an exceptional way just after the second world war. Science opened the way for a development without precedent of new technologies. To this historical phenomenon was added the belief that supply would become something adjustable subsequently to desire. This faith in science and technology, at the same time both new and magic, reached its height in the 1960s. At that time supply seemed unlimited: there were more people working in laboratories and on new technologies than there had been scientists and engineers since the beginning of humanity. The final period of the Industrial Revolution exploded in a display of fireworks. The possibilities of production were extended to a point such that the hypothesis which had become axiom on supply (cope with scarcity in our economic world) disappeared. In this extremely elastic situation of supply the number one economic problem, in particular between the 1930s and the 1970s, was to regulate and stimulate consumption, that is to say demand. It was only in the 1973 crises that the limits of elasticity of the Western system of production were realised.

The rigidity of supply

Three factors explain the structural rigidity of supply: quantitative, qualitative and social. First, the qualitative factors of supply rigidity are closely linked to the decreasing return of technolgy observed in many sectors. In spite of the new technologies in fields such as telecommunications and electronics, which permit a permanent growth in productivity as well as in the creation of new jobs, we are far from the growth in output attained during the Industrial Revolution in *all* the manufacturing sectors. Indeed, at that time, technology not only opened up unexpected possibilities of development in new fields (for example industrial chemistry), but also gave a significant push to the field of industrial mass production.

Today, the iron and steel, textile and extraction industries which were the driving elements behind this whole economic process, are going through serious problems of readaptation and quantitative readjustment. The proof lies in the noticeable drop in the total number of 'industrial' jobs available in Europe and the United States during the last 30 years.

Secondly, the move of an industrial society towards a service is at the root of one of the often most significant rigidities of supply: when more than 80 per cent of production costs are channelled towards service functions which guarantee accessibility to the product on the market, one can state that the old remedies used at production level to relaunch the economy are out of date. Nowadays, any economic recovery will necessarily be a result of improvement in these service functions. Yet, these services are seen as barriers to the spreading of all that characterises new economic development. It is necessary to reverse this tendency in order to concentrate effort where the 80 per cent of production costs are to be found that is, service functions. It is a challenge which economists must take up.

Thirdly, social and political conditions represent further factors of rigidity. Often production activity is limited by financial laws or state intervention. This last factor represents one of the main arguments of the American school of supply-siders. Yet this liberal argument is historically refutable: during periods of great technological progress, innovations have always managed to bypass social and political restrictions. The development of social security systems for the elderly, for accidents or illness, for example, has led to a stimulation of demand in a situation of great supply elasticity. If today such social development is in economic crisis, it is precisely because supply no longer has that infinite elasticity in terms of manufacturing production potential. In the years to come, the objective will have to be an improvement in the use of scarce resources of all sorts (material, non-material, monetarised and non-monetarised). Reducing scarcity and increasing wealth, today, depend much more on the irreproachable working and constant improvement of service functions rather than a simple growth in production. It is no longer sufficient to produce meat and potatoes if there is no appropriate place to store them; if their conservation is not guaranteed; if the distribution network is not adapted.

The paradox of a world where in certain regions extraordinary agricultural surpluses are being produced while there is famine in other parts, presents a formidable challenge, this time, to the whole of humanity. There is not the slightest doubt that getting rid of such differences will be through the development of service activities. It is therefore necessary to re-evaluate the importance of the production of service activities. As has already been seen, this importance is not exclusive. However, it is part of a time dimension different from that which predominated during periods of exceptional growth, and it has new economic agents.

The producer-consumer (prosumer), the supply of service, the external-isation process, self-service

We have described supply in the contemporary economy as a complex system integrating tools, services and service functions, the aim of which is to give a result or an economic value based on the utilisation of goods produced in this way.

A new concept has now become a part of the definition of utilisation value: that of the producer consumer, that is to say the contribution of the consumer himself to the process of production [Norman, 1984: ch.6]. This is what Alvin Toffler [1980] has called the 'prosumer'. There are two identifiable aspects in the concept of 'prosumer': a monetarised and non-monetarised aspect. The first can be illustrated by a simple example where the utiliser (owner) of a computer invests money not only on purchasing the machine, but also on learning how to use it.

The second aspect covers the quality and the non-monetary form to create a utilisation value. Keeping a room, a hospital, a tourist site, or a washing machine in good order is a non-monetarised form of qualitative investment on a product. Thus self-service activity represents another sector in which the 'prosumer' contributes to the creation of an economic value of utilisation by substituting the paid activity with his own activity. Carrying one's own crockery and cutlery in a self-service restaurant corresponds to being an unpaid waiter. Whatever the type of 'self-service shop' it has an activity whose aim is to maximise the economic value of utilisation to a level of cost and effort input, monetary or non-monetary.

One of the characteristics of the service economy is the constant dichotomy between the processes of internal production and the processes of external production requiring an outside economic agent (firm, subsidiary, State, consumer group etc.). The services of a lawyer, a doctor or an insurance agent may exist within the firm producing a given article or service (internal service functions). The same services may, however, be separated from the firm and obtained ouside it (external service functions).

The choice between these two production methods often depends on the advantage of one over the other when generating non-monetary activities. But this is not the general case and the phenomenon is not always new. The main difference lies in the frequency of this dichotomy as well as the great flexibility required for these two production methods to adapt to the conditions of utilisation of the goods produced. From that moment the 'prosumer' finds himself at the centre of a new tendency, that of arriving at his own utilisation value of the acquired object. This new economic agent represents one of the characteristics which in fact offset the structural rigidities of typical production in the 1960s.

In this entirely new situation, it becomes essential for our system of contemporary production (that is to say for the organisation of tools and people in a given environment making it possible to obtain economic results), to take into account its own levels of complexity and vulnerability.

INTEGRATION AND VULNERABILITY

The growth of complexity from the Industrial Revolution to our modern information society

In the first part of the Industrial Revolution, one of the main priorities was to increase production in a relatively specialised environment. During the period of expansion the industrial economy became complex in a vertical and horizontal way. By vertical integration is meant a multitude of the different stages of the transformation of the raw material into a finished product. As for horizontal integration, this concerns above all the whole range of service activities which act as an essential support to the production process. Let us first consider vertical integration.

The consequence of specialisation is to limit the field of application of each new product, and of each new machine meant as a replacement for an obsolete one. In this way the increase in productivity which is obtained is often offset by a decrease in the general potential of a product on the market. The product is becoming specialised. For example, it was possible to use the first weaving looms either for wool or for cotton and manufacture either clothes or bedcovers. Nowadays weaving looms are limited to one type of fibre and one type of clothing. Each step in the production chain is tending towards a specialised transformation needing its own tool equipment. This can be shown in a conclusive manner when decreasing restrictions (technical and financial) makes the improvement of this transformation possible. Thus, specialisation means a multiplication of means and methods which adapt to more and more precise scenarios. For each new technology, the number for intermediate transformation stages has to be increased.

At this point of reflection we can already state that there is a certain degree of specialisation to be optimised beyond which all linear development of specialisation becomes economically negative. Hence the degree of specialisation is linked to fixed objectives and a specialisation strategy can be imagined in which its interest would become insignificant, even zero, because it is badly optimised.

This process of vertical integration has gone together with a development of service activities (horizontal integration) such as insurance, stock mangement, research, training, finance, marketing, security, waste recycling. At the beginning of the Industrial Revolution, most of these service functions already existed: they were considered as non-identifiable, non-classifiable and completely secondary. The production of a small independent artisan posed problems of storage and waste, but to a very small extent and calling for no specialised job to be created. Over the last two hundred years the concentration of the textile industry from small workshops to huge production centres created new professional tasks like stock control and distribution. In terms of risk analysis, this industrial concentration posed the problem of risk coverage. A risk is more easily insurable if its average cost is low and its frequency is higher. As specialisation increases, so more numerous measures will have to be taken to ensure the easy flow of used materials.

Whereas the baker can, if he wishes, buy his flour daily for his daily production, a synthetic fibre factory must have the necessary supply of raw material a long time in advance. A third dimension must be added to the integration process which nowadays is becoming particularly significant, and this is the necessity to co-ordinate all the stages of production. In other words the corollary of this horizontal and vertical integration of economic activity is now the vital need for information, co-ordination and organis-ation at all production levels. The economy becomes a system, or rather a network of growing complexity. This complexity may appear rudimentary or embryonic compared with a real biological system. Nevertheless, contemporary economics must be seen as a network where each component must be able to fit in with the others. This view of the economy also makes it possible to appreciate better the contributions of modern technology whose influence greatly affects the economic system because modern technology is important in the fields of communication, and information organisation. This is different from the role of classical technology, the aim of which was to explore and improve the various production stages which transformed raw products into finished products.

The contemporary economy can therefore be defined as a service economy in the following way: the factors of production are channelled towards service functions. This channelling is only effective thanks to the storage, transmission and processing of information. At this stage notions of risk management and vulnerability become economic notions of the utmost importance.

The uncertainty and vulnerability of systems

The notion of a system becomes essential in the service economy. When correctly working every system has a positive result (or economic value).

Furthermore its correct working can only be seen in time, over a length of time. N. Georgescu-Roegen [1971] calls this period 'continuous time' or 'real time'. Once real time is taken into account then the slightest 'ounce' of uncertainty which might influence man's actions becomes an all-important factor.

During the Industrial Revolution reflection on the economy could be based on the concepts of 'perfect equilibrium' in turn based on the hypothesis of certainty where time and length of time had no role to play. Throughout the history of this way of thinking, risk and uncertainty were only marginal subjects for study and then only perhaps of interest to historians or sociologists.

Any system which aims at getting results is by definition in a situation of uncertainty, even if different situations are characterised by different levels of risk. But the existence of risk and uncertainty leaves no choice, they are part of the human system. From this it can be seen that nationalisation does not mean getting rid of risk or avoiding uncertainty but rather controlling risk, bringing uncertainty and levels of indetermination to acceptable levels in given situations.

To sum up, the profoundly systematic nature of our modern economy, and the growing level of technological complexity, increasingly calls for an understanding and control of vulnerability of the mentioned systems. Unfortunately, the notion of vulnerability is generally misundertood. The statement which claims that vulnerability grows with the increase in qualitative performance of modern technology seem to be a paradox. Indeed the high performance level of all leading technologies is correlated with a decrease in acceptable error margins for that technology. Opening a door of a moving car does not necessarily lead to an accident. There would, however, be an accident were this to happen in a plane. This example goes to show that the concepts of checking vulnerability and analysing the situation have an obvious economic interest, something on which economists and engineers must get together.

CONCLUSION

None of the great classical economists have tackled risk analysis. Risk was an implicit part of the cultural background of the era and Schumpeter hardly made any reference to it in 'The entrepreneur taking risks'. It was only in 1921 that Frank Knight wrote the first comprehensive work entitled *Risk Uncertainty and Profit*. But once again the risks analysed were only of the 'entrepreneur's risks' type. The notion of pure risk directly linked to the notion of vulnerability of the system was once again considered of marginal interest for firm management. Only recently have economists like Kenneth Arrow begun to look realistically at the uncertainty which exists behind every political economic or management decision.

Smith and Ricardo illustrated their theories with practical examples taken from small-sized firms, and the following generation of economists up to Samuelson used real situations taken from large industries. Today, modern economists are taking as indicators of contemporary economics. the management of risk and uncertainty in institutions such as insurance, sectors of public health or other service activities.

The entrepreneur in a service economy must be prepared to tackle new conditions of production which are particular to a more and more complex environment. Even the most prestigious universities and management schools teach nothing or very little of the notions of integration or complexity and vulnerability whereas in the daily working life of managers they are called on to accept the heavy cost of risk.

All risks must be identified as much as possible. Vulnerability must be diminished. A new production strategy must come out of this with new challenges to take up. If this new outlook on economic life is not noticed or lived by the entrepreneur or the general public then the feeling of helplessness when faced with risk and vulnerability will grow, and with it the cultural incapacity to identify and accept everyday reality.

This is therefore a clear question of the attitude to adopt. This cultural incapacity leads to pessimism and fatalistic attitudes in the same way as a sailor allows himself to be carried on by the wind rather than decide on the speed his boat is to adopt. It is necessary to identify the new winds blowing on the service economy. It must be recognised how the challenge of new risks in fact offers the opportunity of fixing new directions and actions to take to go in the direction of real economic and social growth. This growth depends more and more on the quality of the product sold and its utilisation value.

NOTES

1. See Jacques Nusbaumer [1984]. The author gives the example of the cost breakdown of the retail price of margarine in the United States (as a percentage of the whole): Farmer (manure, grain, chemical products, etc. . .) 26.5 per cent storage in silos 0.6 per cent, sorting and loading 2.4 per cent, production (labour, machines, storage, delivery) 25.9 per cent distribution (market research, packing, publicity, transport) 21 per cent, supermarket 23.5 per cent. Only 27 per cent of the cost of margarine can be put down to pure production.
2. For a complete definition of the concept of entropy, see N. Georgescu-Roegen [1971], and Giarini and Louberge [1979].

REFERENCES

Barcet, A., and J. Bonamy, 1986, 'La productivité dans les services, prospective et limite d'un concept', paper presented at Geneva: Deuxièmes Journées Annuelles d'Etudes sur l'Economie de Service, I.U.E.E., June.

Edvinsson, L., 1986, 'The New Business Focus', paper presented at Geneva: Deuxièmes Journées Annuelles d'Etudes sur l'Economie de Service, I.U.E.E., June.

Fourastie, J., 1958, Le Grand Espoir du XXème Siècle, Paris: Gallimard.

Gadrey, J., 1986, 'Productivité, output médiat et immédiat des activités de services: les difficultés d'un transfert de concepts,' paper presented at Geneva: Deuxième Journées Annuelles d'Etudes sur l'Economie de Service, I.U.E.E., June.

Georgescu-Roegen, N., 1971, *The Entropy Law and the Economic Process,* Boston, MA: Harvard University Press.

Gershuny, J., and I. Miles, 1983, *The New Service Economy,* London: Frances Pinter.

Giarini, O. and H. Loubergé, 1979, *Les rendements décroissants de la technologie.* Paris: Dunod.

Leveson, I., 1985, 'The Service Economy in Economic Development', paper presented at Geneva: Institut Universitaire d'Etudes Européennes, April.

Mill, J.S., 1871, *Principles of Political Economy,* reprint, London: Routledge & Kegan Paul, 1968.

Normann, R., 1984, *Service Management, Strategy and Ledershi in Service Business,* New York: John Wiley and Sons.

Nusbaumer, J., 1984, *Les services, nouvelle donne de l'économie,* Paris: Economica.

Riddle, D., 1986, *Service-Led Growth,* New York: Praeger.

Shelp, R.K., 1981, *Beyond Industrialization,* New York: Praeger.

Smith, A., 1776, *The Wealth of Nations,* reprint London: Penguin, 1977.

Toffler, A., 1980, *The Third Wave,* New York: Collins.

The Double Dynamics of Services

by

Jean Gadrey

This article assesses, on a mainly statistical basis, the macro-economic trends of the final consumption of goods and services by households in France and in the USA, and the proportion of services intended for French producers. Its conclusions reveal the existence of double dynamics in the development of services. Some common factors account for this double growth: the complementary nature of goods and services, the growing complexity of production and consumption, the rise of risks to be prevented, and the emergence of new relations between production and use: the social relationships of services.

INTRODUCTION

If there is general agreement, and it is difficult to imagine there is not on the relative growth of services in developed industrial economies, there is however disagreement on the factors leading to this growth and above all, on its prospects and on the types of services which are seen as helping economic development.

There are various theories concerning these interpretations and perspectives. On the one hand the theories of self-service and substitution of goods and services at the final consumer stage herald a stagnation followed by drop in services for households. These ideas are explicitly opposed to the theory of a post industrial society, or a service society, which would gradually replace the industrial society and where personal, collective, cultural and social services would be the priority. There are shades between these extremes, where theories such as the one of Stanback [1979] put the emphasis on the transformations of 'how we produce/what we produce' and on the exceptional dynamics of services to producers.

Therefore it is not without interest to attempt to make a macro-economic diagnosis of this apparent opposition, if only to answer the question: when trying to make an analysis of individual and collective services to households, will we be studying a dying phenomenon or rather a fully growing one? Empirical investigation would now seem necessary and has been carried out on two levels: first, the relative consumption of goods and services by households over the last 15 years; second, the final destination of services in so far as national statistics make it possible for this to be evaluated.

In the first case, the approach will be from the final *demand* and its structure of goods/services. In the second case the approach is on the level of the *supply* of services and its breakdown into services for industry, public authorities and households. This double approach makes it possible to diagnose a double dynamic element in the need for service and to draw up a theoretical arrangement suggesting that care should be taken as far as unilateral theses are concerned. The case study and figures are based on the French economy from 1970 to 1985 and partly on that of the United States from 1965 to 1984.

CONSUMPTION OF GOODS AND SERVICES IN FRANCE, 1970-85

Figure 1 gives the evolution of the volume of household consumption, according to five sub-headings: foodstuffs, consumer durables (including cars), semi-durables (eg., crockery, textiles, leather goods, glassware, plastic goods, tyres etc.) non-durables and non-foodstuffs (other goods) and services. It can clearly be seen that compared with the whole of consumption of goods and services, the relative amount of service consumption has been growing steadily since 1971 *and the gap has even been widening since 1979.*

Precise figures (from National Statistics) are shown in Table 1.

It is therefore natural, given that there was a drop in 1979, to break down the analysis into two sub-periods: 1970-79 and 1979-85. For each of these periods the average annual rate of variation in consumption was taken.

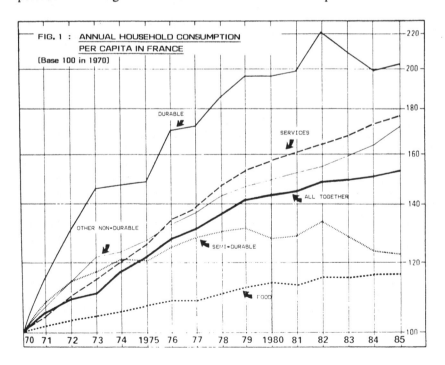

FIG. 1 : ANNUAL HOUSEHOLD CONSUMPTION PER CAPITA IN FRANCE
(Base 100 in 1970)

TABLE 1

HOUSEHOLD CONSUMPTION BY TYPE OF PRODUCT

	Consumption en millions FF		Budgetary ratio		Rate of annual variation (%)				
	1970	1985	1970	1985	1982	1983	1984	1985	Moyenne 1970-1985
1. Durable goods	34 295	224 765	7,3	7,5	10,6	− 3,8	− 6,7	3,1	5,4
of :									
Cars	11 464	86 452	2,4	2,9	19,6	− 1,3	− 13,8	8,3	3,9
T.V. and radio sets	3 044	15 707	0,6	0,5	10,7	− 3,9	2,0	0,6	10,0
Refridgerators, washing machine, dish washer	2 460	9 300	0,5	0,3	7,9	− 7,8	− 5,1	− 0,2	3,4
2. Semi-durables goods............	71 669	356 886	15,3	12,0	3,2	− 2,6	− 3,4	− 0,7	2,0
3. Non durables goods	197 684	1 162 857	42,1	39,0	1,2	1,9	1,5	1,2	2,7
Foodstuffs	120 192	588 568	25,6	19,7	1,0	0,9	0,8	0,7	1,6
Other non durables goods......	77 492	574 289	16,5	19,2	1,5	3,0	2,2	3,5	4,2
4. Services...................	165 442	1 239 905	35,3	41,5	2,9	2,0	2,8	2,2	4,4
TOTAL CONSUMPTION FOR THE COUNTRY	469 090	2 984 413	100,0	100,0	2,9	0,9	0,7	1,9	3,5

FIGURE 2

AVERAGE ANNUAL RATE OF VARIATION, AT CONSTANT PRICES

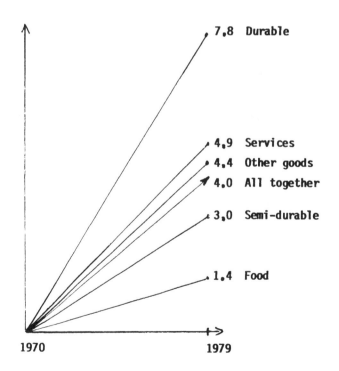

FIGURE 3

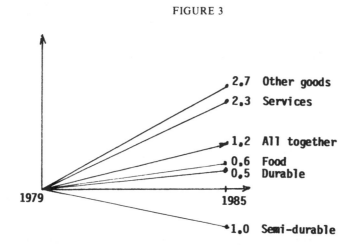

The increase in the consumption of durable goods over services which had been apparent during the 1970s, has now been severely put in doubt since the early 1980s, and the question is therefore whether this is a relative saturation of the present style of consumption concerning these categories of items (which had been at the heart of the previous growth of industrial societies), or whether this is a sign of a newly maturing style of consumer goods (less durable?) which is likely to take over. Whatever the answer, services, although subject to the general slowing down of final consumption, have been widening the gap during the second period as far as the overall variational rate of final consumption is concerned.

Finally it should be stressed that:

- spending on house buying, considered in the national statistics as household investment and not as spending on finished goods, has not been taken into account in the figures and tables shown. However, it is well known that spending on house buying as a proportion of disposable income has been decreasing for some years, which further supports the diagnosis of relative growth in service spending.
- the emphasis here has been put on statistics at constant prices (i.e., volume) but it would be just as useful to point out that consumer value coefficients evolve in an even more advantageous way for services. A study of the case in the USA will help to bring out this element.

THE CASE OF THE UNTED STATES, 1965–84

This second case will be limited to the evolution of the two coefficients:
1. The part α of spending on services in final consumption given in current money.

2. The same relation in constant prices (dollars 1972) representing the 'amount' ß of services consumed as against the total 'amount' of final consumption.

These calculations, based on the 'Statistical Abstract of the US' (1985 edition) and 'Survey of Current Business' (July 1985), give the following results:

TABLE 2

	1965	1970	1975	1980	1984
α = % of spending on services in current money	41.6	43.6	44.8	47.1	49.8
β = % of spending on services at constant prices	43.2	44.6	46.1	47.1	46.2

It can therefore be seen that there is a steady and definite increase in the coefficient α, which has now reached practically 50 per cent: households are spending in proportion more and more on services. However contrary to the French example, coefficient ß dropped slightly between 1980 and 1984 meaning that the 'amount' of services consumed increased more slowly during that period than the quantity of goods consumed.

One point needs to be made concerning the findings: in dealing with the relative demand for goods and services, coefficient α seems to be more pertinent than coefficient ß, both at the micro-economic level (where it shows clearly the choice of households concerning the spending of their income) and at the macro-economic level (where it shows better the effective demand and its influence on related jobs). This seems all the more true in that the overall measurement of the quantities of services 'in constant money terms' raises considerable difficulties of interpretation as is widely known.

THE APPROACH ACCORDING TO THE DESTINATION OF SERVICES

The above figures give no indication as to the place occupied by producer services in the dynamics of services or in general thought on the duality of goods and services.

According to the theory of Gershuny for example, these services are classified together with goods, in so far as they contribute to their production, and they appear as the main factor of tertiary growth. On the other hand the theory of the post-industrial society tends to miss out this aspect of the service society.

The following exercise on statistics aims to give more precise elements of diagnosis for France. Following the work of Greenfield [1966], an evaluation for the whole of the main service industries (T_{29} to T_{38} in the French listing called NAP 40) is made of the fraction of the value produced in each industry which can be considered as being destined for the productive system. In all the cases except three, this imputation was carried out from the coefficients α_i as follows:

$$\alpha_i = \frac{\text{intermediate use (in value) of the product of}}{\text{total uses (intermediate and final) of products i}}$$

The three particular cases are trade, services of financial institutions, and non-marketed services. Unfortunately the methods used by, and the data obtained from, national statistics do not make it possible to break down, in so far as:

- trade is not considered as an input of productive industries, nor as a 'product' in the input-output table. Only the trade margins concerning products are in the main available:
- services of financial institutions are not 'broken down' and it is not possible to evaluate their intermediate output by the productive system from national statistics:
- non-marketed services (branch T_{38}) are (in France) by convention attributed completely to final consumption.

The solutions used for estimating (over the period 1970–83) the fraction of the value obtained from these three industries, which can be considered as being destined for the production system, as opposed to other uses (household, non-trading organisations, general administrative authorities), are as follows:

Trade has been divided into two unequal parts based on manpower distribution between the wholesale and retail trades, the former being considered essentially as destined to the production system, and the latter mainly to households and other units. As the ratio between the two has changed little over the period, an average coefficient has been applied systematically (36 per cent of the accounted trade product thus being considered as destined for the production system).

The services of financial institutions were simply divided into two equal parts, (for this point using Greenfield's assumptions). Such an attitude would be unacceptable within the framework of a specific research on this industry, but, for the overall evaluations proposed here, there is nothing scandalous. It can be noted in fact that the input–output tables for the American economy, better detailed than French input–output entries, showed for 1977 a final consumption of banking and insurance services equal to 3.6 per cent of the national product, and an intermediate use of these services equal to 3.1 per cent of this product [Survey of Current Business: 1984].

Furthermore, both the BLS estimations in terms of jobs per functions as well as these of the French Association of Banks in terms of cost, arrive at close figures [Petit 1984].

Within the non-marketed services, the number of Civil Servants in ministries and institutions aimed at industry, trade, agriculture, economy and budget, work and transport, have been compared with all government employees. The average coefficient (12.5 per cent) thus obtained was then systematically applied to the measurement, by national statistics, of the total value of the non-marketed services.

These conventions (different from those of Greenfield, for whom about a third of public services could be considered as being destined for the producers) are highly debatable but, as we shall see, changing them would not have much effect on the conclusions of this article. They could be improved upon, but the fundamental ambiguities, which are not statistical but theoretical, would remain. Indeed the very concept of *destination* has its limits, especially in the case of services where it is not always possible to identify clearly the social category of destination, especially when these activities have a regulatory function in the social and economic relations between these categories, of general territorial security, etc. One of the reasons for which some services cannot become marketable is precisely because it is impossible to determine their precise destination or buyer.

Returning to statistics, for the three years 1970, 1978 and 1983 and for the industries T_{29} to T_{38} (plus trade, by measure of convention) the following variables have been calculated:

CI_m = value of the intermediate use by the business industries of the product of each service industry.

CI_s = value of the intermediate use by all service industries of the product of each service industry.

α_m^i = ratio, for industry i, of CI_m and the total (T) of its destination (and the same for α_m, the overall relation for all the services).

α_s^i = similar relation concerning CI_s (and the same for α_s).

The results are given in Table 3.

Certain indications can be seen from reading these figures:

1. These results confirm the impression of quantitative stability (for the period under study) of the proportions in which services are used or consumed by the large sectors of economic activity. Since 1970 about a third of the product of the services is used by the business industries and this proportion has not changed. This calls for revision of the theses which consider the exceptional growth in services consumed by the producing sectors as the principal explanation of tertiary vitality. In fact, this productive 'destination' has shown real growth, although more or less parallel, in value, compared to the whole of tertiary growth. Even the branch (T_{33}) of typically producer services has seen the total of its destination, in value, in increase at a rate only slightly higher than the overall rate.

2. The growing need of services for the very activity of services, in intermediate uses, is often forgotten in favour of the privileged links

TABLE 3

Uses of services Service industries	1970 (Billions FF)					1978					1984				
	CI_m	CI_s	T	$\alpha_m I(0/0)$	$\alpha_s I(0/0)$	CI_m	CI_s	T	$\alpha_s I(0/0)$	$\alpha_m I(0/0)$	CI_m	CI_s	T	$\alpha_m I(0/0)$	$\alpha_s I(0/0)$
T_{25} to T_{28} : trade	8,8	4,4	24,6	36	18	20	14	78	36	18	50	25	139	36	18
T_{29} Car repair and sales	5,3	3,3	16,6	31,9	19,8	18	12,3	50	36	24,6	38	26,6	107	36,6	24,9
T_{30} Hotel and catering services	5,6	4,9	37,3	15	13,1	13,6	12,1	96	14,2	12,6	31	27,3	203	15,3	13,4
T_{31} Transport	38,2	22	61,9	61,7	35,6	107	66,4	175	61,1	37,9	184	116	329	55,9	35,3
T_{32} Post and Telecom.	8,5	7,9	13,5	63	58,5	34	30,4	50	68	60,8	63	58,1	101	62,4	57,5
T_{33} Other marketed services to firms	50	24,6	74,1	67,5	33,2	152	74,3	232	65,5	32	318	161	490	64,9	32,9
T_{34} Other marketed services to individuals (including health)	5,9	5,7	57,1	10,3	10	19	18,2	190	10	9,6	42	39,3	403	10,4	9,7
T_{35} Real estate	4,8	4,5	49,7	9,7	9,1	15	13,4	143	10,5	9,4	31	29,6	298	10,4	9,9
T_{36} Insurance	4,2	2,2	9,8	42,9	22,4	9	5,2	24	37,5	21,7	9	5,6	32	28,1	17,5
T_{37} Financial institutions	12,7	6,3	25,4	50	25	44	22	88	50	25	101	50	203	50	25
T_{38} Non-marketed services and government	14	7	112,6	12,5	6,2	43	21,5	342	12,6	6,2	85	42	679	12,5	6,2
TOTAL	158	92,8	482	32,8	19,2	483	290	1 468	31,6	19,7	952	580	2 984	31,9	19,4

Note: In evaluating CI_s, conventions are also needed in three cases: trade, financial institutions and non-marketed services. The solution consists of retaining for these three industries a proportion $\frac{CI_s}{CI_m}$ equal to that of industry T_{33} (services to firms); this happens to give a coefficient of 50 per cent.

between manufacturing and services. Indeed industries such as trade, transport, telecommunications, and marketed services are great consumers of services. The coefficients $\alpha_{\dot{s}}$ and α_s reflect this dimension of the use of services by other services. It is moreover possible to give global idea of this importance by comparing the total amount of the use of intermediate services by the tertiary sector, and then by both the primary and secondary sectors together. The following figures are thus obtained:

- In 1970 respectively: 92.8 and 101.7 billion FF (current prices)
- In 1978: 290 and 286 billion FF.
- In 1983: 580 and 562 billion FF.

As a result, over this period, services overtook all of the other industries concerning the use of services, in absolute value. As regards services to firms (branch T_{33}), 45.6 per cent of ther destination took place in 1983 in services (42.8 per cent in 1970).

3. These global estimates can be specified according to various branches, from destination coefficients $\alpha_{\dot{m}}$ and $\alpha_{\dot{s}}$. On the whole, they are also quite stable the most noticeable changes concerning the branches T_{29} (car repair and trade, for which the productive use increased during the 1970s), T_{31} and T_{32} (transport and telecommunications, for which the coefficients of productive use have dropped since 1978 mainly in manufacturing), and T_{36} (insurance, which has undergone a large drop of this coefficient).

Two remarks must be made about this statistical exercise: first, it should not be mistaken for the analysis of traditional Leontief coefficients of service purchase *by* various industries of the economy, and second, it is based on values (in current price terms) of intermediate and final use, these two elements only making up one of the ways of tackling a quantitative study of the destinations of services. It is considered all the same that in the present state of statistical sources, this adequately reflects the relative economic importance and the amount of work supplied and implicitly exchanged.

Note that a similar exercise, based on the input–output tables of the US economy, for the services classified from 65 to 79 in the usual 85-line classification shows that the ratio

$$\frac{\text{intermediate uses of services in business industries}}{(\text{intermediate uses}) + (\text{personal consumption of those services})}$$

increased slightly from 42.3 per cent in 1977 to 44.8 per cent in 1981. Government services are not taken into account in this calculation.

THE ARTICULATION OF THESE TWO DYNAMICS

If it is important to evaluate what, in the present growth in services, goes repectively to intermediate and final demand, it is not sufficient to stop at this dualistic approach – statistics based on a functional breakdown of services cannot be confused with a causal analysis. For example, it seems clear that a part of services to firms (e.g. marketing, publicity) has greatly increased because of the complexity and diversification of the final demand, something that firms will have to know with more and more precision. Conversely some of the services for households are developing on the basis of changes in productive organisations which, for example, are beginning to propose 'compounds' of goods and services (e.g. maintenance, insurance, after-sales) and not only simple goods which finish their shelf or selling life at the moment of purchase.

In more general terms, if it seems that the demand for services is so strongly noticeable in final consumption as well as in intermediate consumption, it is probably because common and comparable technical factors, economic and social, are at play *in both cases*. The articulation of these two dynamics consists therefore of isolating these factors and, in order to advance in that direction, particular attention will be drawn to four of them: *the complementarity* of the use of goods and services within 'compounds' or withing functions; the growing social and technical *complexity* of production closely associated with the 'demassification' of demand and/or the correlating development of information activities; the necessity for *continuity* of the working of the systems and dominating the corresponding risks, and, more generally stating, *the social relations of services* integrating the production and consumption of the results of the activities.

These four general factors are both technical and social, according to variable proportions.

I. *The complementarity of the use of goods and services and the subordination of objects to functions*

This characteristic comes from observing the present conditions of the use of goods and services by economic units (households, firms, administrations). It value has been pointed to by various authors, namely Stanback and research workers in New York, but also, as regards services to firms, by followers of the functional approach to these activities. All of these researchers consider that the unities of commodities tend no longer to be defined at the level of objects, but rather as complex associations of goods and complementary services.

Three points can be made here:

1.   The question of the direction of this complementarity is not always explicitly dealt with, but is more often represented as coming from the use of goods, and not the the other way round. Goods remain at the heart of the explanation. Yet, situations are increasing where 'software', which has become strategic *vis-à-vis* 'hardware', domintes the demand for the latter.

2.   The complementarity can be immediate in cases where the use of the goods and services is simultaneous (the provision of services, for

example, generally have goods as supports, which are used and consumed when supplying the service). It can be mediate or indirect, in the cases where the purchase of goods is the motive for a later demand in services (e.g. maintenance, insurance), or inversely (health services leading to a demand for goods).

3.   Finally, it can be even more distant, when not only the complementarity in final consumption is called into play, but also the strategies of producers; indeed, for example, the power of multinational computer and telecommunications firms can influence promotion in a country's creation (e.g. music, cinema, culture). There is then no longer only complementarity of use but interactivity of the production structures of goods and services.

The theoretical use of the concept of 'function' poses complex methodological problems, the principle of which is that functions are not eternal, they also change, and new functions appear. In particular, the main technical functions used in classifications must be broken down into social functions sufficiently fine so that analyses of complementarity or substitutability may be evaluated. For example, the technical function 'transport of people' is not of much theoretical help until the main *social motives* of this transport have been defined.

The complementarity of goods and services concerns the final demand just as much as intermediate use. Its analysis is certainly useful when attempting to understand how the services develop. However, observation of this does not make it possible to answer the question, why, within the framework of this complementarity, do services seem to be playing an increasing role? Therefore it is necesary to bring in other explanations, taking as their source the changes in the structures of production and consumption.

II. *Complexity of production, diversification of demand, economics of information*

Here again it is necessary to compare observations with the interpretations of existing theories, in order to bring out the tendencies and produce new or more precise explanations.

The main factor of growing needs for services, a characterisation of which is made here, is present in Stanback's theory based on simultaneous changes in the producing and consuming functions (how we produce/what we produce) and in the analyses by Toffler of the 'demassification' of these two spheres of activity and the speeding up of the rate of change.

The services appear then, explicitly [Stanback 1970] or implicitly [Toffler 1979], as regulating and controlling activities of the technical or social complexity, of simultaneous management of more variables, both at micro-economic and macro-economic levels. This is why it is possible to associate with these factors the notion of information and the theses which see in the information activities the dominant form both of new industry and of services.

In the same way as with the previous concepts of complementarity or of function, extreme theoretical prudence is necessary in the use of these stimulating but vague notions of information or complexity. In particular, those activities which deal with coded and standardised information, and which consequently lend themselves to an intensified automation of their procedures, have a development logic different from those based on the relationship, training and advice, the exchange and adaptation of knowledge. This is why it is necessary to attempt to go further than just the technical dimension of information to envisage the reasons for using information type services. Among these reasons, the requirements of the continuous working of systems and risk management seem to take up an ever-growing space.

III. *The continuity of systems and the economics of risk*

Reference is made here to the theses of Giarini [1986] partly supported by those mentioned above but emphasising an important dimension of the economics of complexity: security, controlling, management and covering of risks entailed by the working of systems or units inserted in these systems (individuals, firms, organisations). Such an approach is not only applied to the economics of insurance, but seems to concern many services destined for individuals (public or private services related to health risks, whether social or professional) or for firms trying to master or know their environment better or organise themselves in order to face the risks of technical, economic or social malfunctioning.

Once again the introduction of such a concept seems dependent on a more precise definition of *social categories of risks,* avoiding confusion with, on the one hand, for example, the factors which leads individuals to spend considerable sums on their personal care, and on the other hand, the needs for insurance, control and technical monitoring of giant industries (e.g. nuclear power, chemicals) which could trigger off ecological catastrophes. Furthermore, it is certainly not possible to analyse globally with this category public or private services of education and training, general administration, production and distribution of knowledge. For this reason a different approach is suggested, with a sociological as well as economical dimension, which might group together several of the characteristics of the first three concepts.

IV. *Social relationships of services*

The hypothesis which is made here and which takes in briefly some elements of an earlier paper [Delaunay, Gadrey, Silver, 1986] is that the central element of the new economics of services is not of a technical order, in spite of its obvious technical dimensions, but of a social order, and that it can be defined as a new type of relationship between production (of goods or services) and consumer activities. This calls into question:

- the traditional separation of production and consumption, of supply and demand;
- the classical industrial organisation of work, divided and specialised, especially between designing and manufacturing, thinking and doing.

A different way of producing, consuming and living in society, marked by the trend towards integration and bringing together of spheres previously separated, seems to be the main stakes of the 'service society'.

The main problem met in analysing these tendencies is the following: there is a simultaneous globalisation of the systems of supply and a differentiation of individual demand, a complexification of relationship networks and an integration of tasks at a micro-economic level, as if the main obstacle faced by the developed societies today were in the difficulties of adapting complex and globalised supply systems (final or intermediate) to demassified conditions of use and to the requirements of the users to intervene in the definition of products (goods or services). If there are 'diminishing returns' of the productive system, it is perhaps not in the field of technologies [Giarini, Loubergé, 1978], but at the level of its ability to face up to more creative conditions of use of goods and services, and to corresponding requirements 'of enrichment' of work content. Moreover, services are at the heart of these contradictory processes of bringing together unities and agents of production and consumption, whether they be producer services or the bulk of individual or collective services rendered to households. It does not therefore concern only trends towards 'prosumerism' (according to Toffler) but forms of integration which affect both the organisation of production and that of administrations.

Such an approach does not contradict the previous ones. On the contrary it permits a better comprehension of:

- The factors of the growing complementarity of goods and services, which more often than not result from the social conditions of the use of goods (maintenance, guarantees, trade, information, insurance, control of productive systems). The reasoning in terms of 'functions' precisely make reference to the narrowing gap between production and consumption within the categories of final use.
- The role of the complexity of production facing the differentiation of demand, and of information; indeed these technical characteristics correspond to social processes bringing into relationship the most subtle conditions of use and the corresponding organisation of supply.
- The importance of the risk economy, which can be interpreted from the requirement for a continuity and quality in the use of products (goods or services), both in production and in consumption.

The analysis of services, seen in this way, comes closer therefore to an economy of the use-value and the integration of consumption characteristics from the very outset of production, It is a little as if this necessary association of the two spheres was a means of preventing the growing social risk faced when they function separately.

If this analysis is well-founded, then the service economy has a viable future as long as the industrialist paradigm (which still produces economic analyses) accepts the changes and integrations implied by a reflection on the product and use of services.

REFERENCES

Barcet, A., J. Bonamy and A. Mayere, 1982, *L'économie des services aux entreprises,* Paris: Commissariat Général du Plan.

Delaunay, J.C., J. Gadrey and H. Silver, 1986, *Rethinking Services in France and United States. Seminar 'France-USA',* Paris: Groupe de Sociologie du Travail.

Delaunay, J.C. and J. Gadrey, 1987, *La Société de service.* Paris: Presses de la Fondation Nationale des Sciences Politiques.

Gershuny, J.I., 1983, *Social Innovation and the Division of Labour,* Oxford University Press.

Giarini, O., and H. Louberge, 1978, *The Diminishing Return of Technology* Oxford: Pergamon Press.

Giarini, O., 1986, 'Coming of Age of the Service Economy', *Science and Public Policy.* Vol.13, No.4, August.

Greenfield, H.I., 1966, *Manpower and the Growth Producer Services,* New York: Columbia University Press.

Petit, P., 1984, *Services Automation: The Case of Banking* Paris: Centre d'Etudes prospectives d'Economie Mathématique Appliquées à la planification (C.E.P.R.E.M.A.P.) No. 8431.

Stanback, T.M., 1979, *Understanding the Service Economy* Baltimore: Johns Hopkins University Press.

Survey of Current Business, 1984, US Department of Commerce Bureau of Economic Analysis, Washington DC, May.

Survey of Current Business, 1987, US Department of Commerce Bureau of Economic Analysis, Washington DC, January.

Toffler, A., 1970. *Future Shock,* New York: Random House.